Serious Pie Creations: A Culinary Journey Through 96 Inspired Recipes from Tom Douglas's Iconic Restaurant Menu

Hungry Hippo Haven

Contents

INTRODUCTION

"Serious Pie Creations: A Culinary Journey Through 96 Inspired Recipes from Tom Douglas's Iconic Restaurant Menu" invites you on an extraordinary gastronomic voyage. This cookbook is a treasure trove of 96 tantalizing recipes curated from the acclaimed menu of Tom Douglas's renowned Serious Pie restaurant.

Nestled in the heart of Seattle, Serious Pie has become a culinary beacon, celebrated for its innovative approach to artisanal pizza-making. Tom Douglas, a culinary luminary and James Beard Award-winning chef, has crafted an exquisite collection of dishes that pay homage to the rich tapestry of flavors, textures, and aromas found in the Pacific Northwest.

Within these pages, embark on an epicurean adventure that captures the essence of Serious Pie's culinary artistry. Each recipe is a testament to the restaurant's commitment to using locally sourced, seasonal ingredients, coupled with masterful techniques that elevate pizza-making to an art form. From classic combinations to daring fusions, this cookbook unveils the secrets behind Serious Pie's signature pies that have garnered a devoted following.

Discover the foundation of perfect pizza dough—crisp, yet tender; blistered from the oven, offering a satisfying chew with every bite. Learn the intricate dance of flavors as house-made sauces, ranging from tangy tomato to rich béchamel, intertwine with an array of fresh produce, premium cheeses, and artisanal meats. Delve into the alchemy of the wood-fired oven, where pizzas are transformed into delectable masterpieces, kissed by flames to achieve a sublime balance of textures and tastes.

But Serious Pie Creations offers more than just pizzas. Explore a symphony of flavors beyond the crust with an assortment of starters, salads, and delectable desserts. Indulge in small plates bursting with local ingredients and global influences, enhancing the dining experience with every bite. Elevate your culinary repertoire with savory sides and decadent sweets that complement the main attractions.

The cookbook doesn't merely present recipes; it invites you behind the scenes of Serious Pie's kitchen, sharing insights, tips, and tricks from Chef Tom Douglas himself. With detailed instructions and vivid imagery, aspiring home cooks and seasoned chefs alike can replicate the magic of

Serious Pie in their own kitchens. Whether it's a casual gathering with friends or a special family dinner, these recipes promise to captivate taste buds and create memorable dining experiences.

Furthermore, the book celebrates the ethos of sustainability and community, reflecting Tom Douglas's commitment to supporting local farmers and producers. It's a tribute to the Pacific Northwest's culinary heritage and the vibrant tapestry of cultures that contribute to its vibrant food scene.

"Serious Pie Creations" isn't just a cookbook; it's a culinary passport inviting you to embark on a flavorful expedition through the essence of Serious Pie's menu. It encapsulates the spirit of creativity, passion, and dedication that defines Tom Douglas's iconic restaurant, inspiring home cooks to embrace the artistry of pizza-making and beyond. Get ready to savor the essence of Serious Pie—one recipe at a time.

1. Margherita Pizza

Celebrate the culinary artistry inspired by Tom Douglas's renowned Serious Pie restaurant with this classic Margherita Pizza recipe. A homage to simplicity and flavor, this pizza captures the essence of Italian cuisine with its perfect balance of fresh ingredients. Experience the magic of a thin, crisp crust topped with vibrant tomatoes, creamy mozzarella, and fragrant basil. Transport yourself to the heart of Naples with every savory bite of this iconic dish.

Serving: Makes 2 medium-sized pizzas
Preparation Time: 20 minutes
Ready Time: 15-20 minutes (including baking)

Ingredients:
- 2 1/4 teaspoons active dry yeast
- 1 teaspoon sugar
- 3/4 cup warm water
- 2 cups all-purpose flour
- 1 teaspoon salt
- 2 tablespoons olive oil
- 1/2 cup pizza sauce
- 2 large tomatoes, thinly sliced
- 8 ounces fresh mozzarella, sliced
- Fresh basil leaves, for garnish
- Salt and pepper, to taste

Instructions:
1. Prepare the Dough:
- In a small bowl, combine the yeast, sugar, and warm water. Let it sit for 5-7 minutes until foamy.
- In a large mixing bowl, combine the flour and salt. Make a well in the center and pour in the yeast mixture and olive oil.
- Mix until a dough forms, then knead on a floured surface for about 5 minutes until smooth. Place in a lightly oiled bowl, cover with a damp cloth, and let it rise for 1 hour.
2. Preheat the Oven:

- Preheat your oven to 475°F (245°C). If you have a pizza stone, place it in the oven during preheating.
3. Roll Out the Dough:
- Divide the dough into two portions. On a floured surface, roll out each portion into a thin round shape.
4. Assemble the Pizza:
- Place the rolled-out dough on a pizza peel or parchment paper.
- Spread an even layer of pizza sauce, leaving a small border around the edges.
- Arrange the sliced tomatoes and mozzarella on top. Season with salt and pepper to taste.
5. Bake:
- If using a pizza stone, carefully transfer the pizza onto the hot stone in the oven. Otherwise, place the pizza on a baking sheet.
- Bake for 10-12 minutes or until the crust is golden and the cheese is melted and bubbly.
6. Garnish and Serve:
- Remove the pizza from the oven and let it cool for a minute. Sprinkle fresh basil leaves on top.
- Slice and serve immediately, savoring the delicious simplicity of the Margherita Pizza.

Nutrition Information:
(Per serving - 1/4 of a pizza)
- Calories: 350
- Total Fat: 15g
- Saturated Fat: 6g
- Cholesterol: 30mg
- Sodium: 650mg
- Total Carbohydrates: 40g
- Dietary Fiber: 2g
- Sugars: 2g
- Protein: 15g
Enjoy the authentic flavors of Serious Pie's Margherita Pizza, a timeless classic that brings the essence of Italy to your table.

2. Yukon Gold Potato Pizza

Inspired by the inventive and delicious creations at Tom Douglas's Serious Pie restaurant, this Yukon Gold Potato Pizza is a unique twist on the traditional pizza. The golden Yukon potatoes bring a rich, buttery flavor to each bite, complemented by a medley of carefully selected ingredients. This recipe is a celebration of quality ingredients and the artistry of combining flavors to create a memorable dining experience.

Serving: 4 servings
Preparation Time: 20 minutes
Ready Time: 40 minutes

Ingredients:
- 1 pound pizza dough, homemade or store-bought
- 2 tablespoons olive oil, divided
- 1 clove garlic, minced
- 1 teaspoon fresh rosemary, chopped
- 1 medium-sized Yukon Gold potato, thinly sliced
- 1/2 cup fontina cheese, shredded
- 1/4 cup Parmesan cheese, grated
- Salt and pepper to taste
- Optional: red pepper flakes for a hint of spice

Instructions:
1. Preheat the Oven:
Preheat your oven to 450°F (230°C). If you have a pizza stone, place it in the oven to heat.
2. Prepare the Dough:
Roll out the pizza dough on a floured surface to your desired thickness. If you're using a pizza stone, transfer the rolled-out dough onto a piece of parchment paper.
3. Prepare the Toppings:
a. In a small bowl, mix one tablespoon of olive oil with minced garlic and chopped rosemary.
b. Brush the olive oil mixture evenly over the rolled-out dough.
4. Layer the Potatoes:
Arrange the thinly sliced Yukon Gold potatoes evenly over the dough, slightly overlapping. Drizzle the remaining olive oil over the potatoes, and season with salt and pepper to taste.
5. Add Cheese:

Sprinkle the shredded fontina and grated Parmesan cheese over the potatoes. For an extra kick, you can add red pepper flakes.

6. Bake the Pizza:

If using a pizza stone, carefully transfer the parchment paper with the pizza onto the hot stone. Bake in the preheated oven for about 15-20 minutes or until the crust is golden and the potatoes are cooked through.

7. Finish and Serve:

Once out of the oven, let the pizza cool for a few minutes. Slice and serve hot. The combination of crispy crust, creamy potatoes, and melted cheese makes for a delightful culinary experience.

Nutrition Information:
(Per Serving)
- Calories: 350
- Total Fat: 12g
- Saturated Fat: 4g
- Cholesterol: 15mg
- Sodium: 550mg
- Total Carbohydrates: 50g
- Dietary Fiber: 3g
- Sugars: 2g
- Protein: 10g
Note: Nutritional values are approximate and may vary based on specific ingredients and portion sizes.

3. Sweet Fennel Sausage Pizza

Indulge your taste buds in the delectable world of Tom Douglas's Serious Pie with this Sweet Fennel Sausage Pizza recipe. Inspired by the innovative and bold flavors of the renowned restaurant, this pizza promises a harmonious blend of sweet and savory, punctuated by the distinctive essence of fennel-infused sausage. Elevate your pizza game and embark on a culinary journey that mirrors the mastery of Serious Pie's iconic menu.

Serving: 4 servings
Preparation Time: 20 minutes
Ready Time: 35 minutes

Ingredients:
- 1 pound pizza dough (store-bought or homemade)
- 1/2 cup pizza sauce
- 1 cup shredded mozzarella cheese
- 1/2 cup grated Parmesan cheese
- 1/2 pound sweet fennel sausage, casing removed and crumbled
- 1 medium red onion, thinly sliced
- 1 tablespoon olive oil
- 1 teaspoon red pepper flakes (optional)
- Fresh basil leaves for garnish

Instructions:
1. Preheat your oven to 475°F (245°C).
2. Roll out the pizza dough on a lightly floured surface to your desired thickness. If you prefer a thinner crust, roll it out more, and for a thicker crust, keep it a bit heftier.
3. Transfer the rolled-out dough to a pizza stone or a baking sheet.
4. Spread the pizza sauce evenly over the dough, leaving a small border around the edges for the crust.
5. Sprinkle the shredded mozzarella and grated Parmesan cheese over the sauce.
6. In a skillet over medium heat, add the olive oil and sauté the crumbled sweet fennel sausage until browned and cooked through. Spread the cooked sausage evenly over the pizza.
7. Scatter the thinly sliced red onions over the sausage.
8. Optionally, sprinkle red pepper flakes for an extra kick.
9. Bake in the preheated oven for 15-18 minutes or until the crust is golden brown and the cheese is melted and bubbly.
10. Remove from the oven and let it cool for a few minutes before slicing.
11. Garnish with fresh basil leaves just before serving.

Nutrition Information:
(Per serving)
- Calories: 450
- Total Fat: 20g
- Saturated Fat: 8g
- Cholesterol: 50mg
- Sodium: 900mg

- Total Carbohydrates: 45g
- Dietary Fiber: 2g
- Sugars: 4g
- Protein: 20g

Elevate your pizza experience with the Sweet Fennel Sausage Pizza inspired by the culinary prowess of Tom Douglas's Serious Pie. Perfect for a cozy night in or a gathering with friends, this pizza is a delightful fusion of flavors that will leave your taste buds craving more.

4. Penn Cove Clam Pizza

Indulge in the culinary mastery of Tom Douglas's Serious Pie restaurant with this delectable Penn Cove Clam Pizza. Inspired by the restaurant's commitment to quality and bold flavors, this pizza brings together the freshness of Penn Cove clams with a medley of complementary ingredients, resulting in a symphony of taste on every bite.

Serving: 2-4
Preparation Time: 20 minutes
Ready Time: 30 minutes

Ingredients:
- 1 pound pizza dough, at room temperature
- 2 tablespoons olive oil
- 1 cup shredded mozzarella cheese
- 1 cup fresh ricotta cheese
- 1/2 cup grated Parmesan cheese
- 2 dozen Penn Cove clams, cleaned and steamed
- 3 cloves garlic, thinly sliced
- 1/4 cup fresh parsley, chopped
- Red pepper flakes, to taste
- Salt and black pepper, to taste
- Cornmeal (for dusting)

Instructions:
1. Preheat the Oven:

Preheat your oven to the highest temperature it can go (typically around 475-500°F or 245-260°C). If you have a pizza stone, place it in the oven during the preheating process.

2. Prepare the Clams:

Steam the Penn Cove clams until they open, discarding any that do not open. Remove the clams from their shells, chop them into bite-sized pieces, and set aside.

3. Roll Out the Dough:

Dust your work surface with cornmeal to prevent sticking. Roll out the pizza dough to your desired thickness.

4. Assemble the Pizza:

Place the rolled-out dough on a pizza peel or an inverted baking sheet. Drizzle olive oil over the dough, then evenly spread mozzarella, ricotta, Parmesan, sliced garlic, and the chopped Penn Cove clams. Season with salt, black pepper, and red pepper flakes to taste.

5. Bake the Pizza:

If you have a pizza stone, carefully transfer the pizza onto the preheated stone in the oven. If not, simply place the baking sheet in the oven. Bake until the crust is golden and the cheese is melted and bubbly, about 10-12 minutes.

6. Garnish and Serve:

Remove the pizza from the oven and sprinkle fresh parsley over the top. Slice and serve hot.

Nutrition Information:

Note: Nutritional values may vary based on specific ingredients used and portion sizes.

- Calories: 400 per serving (based on 4 servings)
- Protein: 18g
- Carbohydrates: 45g
- Fat: 18g
- Fiber: 2g
- Sugar: 1g
- Sodium: 800mg

Elevate your pizza experience with the rich flavors of Penn Cove clams, creating a dish that pays homage to the inventive spirit of Tom Douglas's Serious Pie restaurant. Enjoy the delicious union of fresh seafood, cheese, and aromatic herbs in every mouthwatering slice.

5. Roasted Chanterelle Mushroom Pizza

Delight in the earthy essence of roasted chanterelle mushrooms atop a delectable pizza crust inspired by Tom Douglas's Serious Pie restaurant. This recipe celebrates the robust flavors of nature's bounty, creating a harmonious medley that's both rustic and indulgent.

Serving: 2-4 servings
Preparation time: 20 minutes
Ready time: 40 minutes

Ingredients:
- 1 pound pizza dough (store-bought or homemade)
- 2 cups chanterelle mushrooms, cleaned and sliced
- 1 tablespoon olive oil
- 2 cloves garlic, minced
- 1 cup shredded fontina cheese
- 1/2 cup grated Parmesan cheese
- Fresh thyme leaves for garnish
- Salt and pepper to taste
- Cornmeal or flour for dusting

Instructions:
1. Preheat your oven to 475°F (245°C) and place a pizza stone or baking sheet inside to heat up.
2. In a skillet over medium-high heat, add olive oil. Once hot, add the chanterelle mushrooms and sauté until they start to brown, about 5-7 minutes.
3. Add minced garlic to the skillet and sauté for another 1-2 minutes until fragrant. Season with salt and pepper. Remove from heat and set aside.
4. Dust a clean surface with cornmeal or flour. Roll out the pizza dough into a circle or desired shape.
5. Carefully transfer the rolled-out dough to a pizza peel or parchment paper.
6. Sprinkle fontina cheese evenly over the pizza dough, leaving a border for the crust.
7. Spread the sautéed chanterelle mushrooms and garlic mixture over the cheese.
8. Sprinkle grated Parmesan cheese on top.

9. Slide the pizza onto the preheated pizza stone or baking sheet in the oven.

10. Bake for 12-15 minutes or until the crust is golden and the cheese is bubbly and melted.

11. Remove the pizza from the oven and garnish with fresh thyme leaves.

12. Let it cool slightly before slicing, then serve and enjoy!

Nutrition Information: (Approximate values per serving)
- Calories: 380
- Fat: 15g
- Carbohydrates: 45g
- Protein: 15g
- Fiber: 3g

Note: Nutritional values are approximate and may vary based on specific ingredients used and serving sizes.

6. Buffalo Mozzarella Pizza

Welcome to the world of Serious Pie, inspired by the culinary creations of Tom Douglas. One of the standout dishes from Serious Pie's menu is the Buffalo Mozzarella Pizza. This delectable pizza is a celebration of simplicity and quality ingredients, showcasing the richness of buffalo mozzarella combined with the robust flavors of a well-made pizza crust.

Serving: This Buffalo Mozzarella Pizza recipe serves 4.
Preparation time: 20 minutes
Ready time: Approximately 30 minutes

Ingredients:
- 1 pound pizza dough, at room temperature
- 8 ounces buffalo mozzarella, thinly sliced
- 1 cup San Marzano tomato sauce
- Fresh basil leaves, torn
- Extra-virgin olive oil
- Kosher salt
- Freshly ground black pepper
- Red pepper flakes (optional)

Instructions:
1. Preheat your oven to its highest setting, usually around 500°F (260°C). Place a pizza stone or an upside-down baking sheet in the oven to heat.
2. Divide the pizza dough into 4 equal portions. On a lightly floured surface, stretch and shape each portion into a round disc, approximately 8-10 inches in diameter.
3. Spread a thin layer of San Marzano tomato sauce over each pizza dough round, leaving a border around the edges.
4. Arrange the thinly sliced buffalo mozzarella evenly over the sauce.
5. Season the pizzas with a pinch of kosher salt and freshly ground black pepper. If desired, sprinkle red pepper flakes for added heat.
6. Carefully transfer the prepared pizzas onto the preheated pizza stone or baking sheet in the oven.
7. Bake the pizzas for about 10-12 minutes or until the crust is golden brown and the cheese is bubbly and slightly browned.
8. Once out of the oven, drizzle each pizza with a touch of extra-virgin olive oil and scatter torn fresh basil leaves over the top.
9. Allow the pizzas to cool for a minute before slicing and serving.

Nutrition Information (per serving):
- Calories: 380
- Total Fat: 14g
- Saturated Fat: 7g
- Cholesterol: 35mg
- Sodium: 820mg
- Total Carbohydrate: 44g
- Dietary Fiber: 2g
- Sugars: 5g
- Protein: 18g

Enjoy the irresistible blend of flavors in this Buffalo Mozzarella Pizza, a delightful representation of Serious Pie's culinary prowess.

7. Prosciutto & Pear Pizza

Indulge in the tantalizing flavors of Tom Douglas's Serious Pie restaurant with this Prosciutto & Pear Pizza recipe. A harmonious blend of sweet and savory, this dish marries the delicate sweetness of ripe pears with the rich, salty goodness of prosciutto, creating a pizza that's both sophisticated and comforting.

Serving: 2-4 people
Preparation time: 20 minutes
Ready time: 30 minutes

Ingredients:
- 1 pizza dough (store-bought or homemade)
- 2 tablespoons olive oil
- 1 cup shredded mozzarella cheese
- 4 slices of prosciutto
- 1 ripe pear, thinly sliced
- 1/4 cup crumbled gorgonzola or blue cheese
- Freshly ground black pepper
- Arugula (optional, for garnish)

Instructions:
1. Preheat Oven: Preheat your oven to 475°F (245°C). If you have a pizza stone, place it in the oven while it preheats.
2. Prepare Dough: Roll out the pizza dough on a lightly floured surface to your desired thickness. Transfer it to a pizza peel or a baking sheet lined with parchment paper.
3. Assemble Pizza: Brush the rolled-out dough with olive oil, leaving a small border untouched for the crust. Sprinkle the shredded mozzarella evenly over the oiled dough. Arrange the prosciutto slices and pear slices over the cheese. Crumble the gorgonzola or blue cheese on top and finish with a grind of black pepper.
4. Bake: If using a pizza stone, carefully transfer the assembled pizza onto the hot stone in the oven. Otherwise, place the baking sheet with the pizza into the oven.
5. Bake the Pizza: Bake for about 12-15 minutes or until the crust is golden brown, and the cheese is melted and bubbly.
6. Finish and Serve: Once done, remove the pizza from the oven. If desired, garnish with fresh arugula for a peppery bite. Slice and serve hot.

Nutrition Information (per serving, assuming 4 servings):
- Calories: 380
- Total Fat: 18g
- Saturated Fat: 6g

- Cholesterol: 30mg
- Sodium: 840mg
- Total Carbohydrate: 40g
- Dietary Fiber: 3g
- Sugars: 8g
- Protein: 16g

This Prosciutto & Pear Pizza brings together the essence of Serious Pie's innovative and delicious offerings, combining flavors that will delight your taste buds in every bite. Enjoy it as a meal for a cozy night in or share it with friends for a memorable dining experience!

8. Penn Cove Clams with House Pancetta

Indulge in the exquisite flavors of the Pacific Northwest with this delectable recipe inspired by the renowned Serious Pie restaurant by Tom Douglas. Penn Cove Clams with House Pancetta showcases the region's finest ingredients, combining the briny richness of fresh Penn Cove clams with the savory goodness of house-cured pancetta. Elevate your culinary experience with this sophisticated yet approachable dish that captures the essence of Tom Douglas's culinary mastery.

Serving: 4 servings
Preparation Time: 20 minutes
Ready Time: 35 minutes

Ingredients:
- 2 pounds fresh Penn Cove clams, scrubbed and cleaned
- 1/2 pound house-cured pancetta, diced
- 2 tablespoons extra-virgin olive oil
- 4 cloves garlic, minced
- 1 cup dry white wine
- 1 cup cherry tomatoes, halved
- 1/4 cup fresh parsley, chopped
- Salt and black pepper to taste
- Red pepper flakes (optional, for a hint of heat)
- Crusty bread, for serving

Instructions:

1. In a large skillet or deep pan, heat olive oil over medium heat. Add diced pancetta and cook until it becomes crispy and golden brown, approximately 5 minutes.

2. Add minced garlic to the pan and sauté for 1-2 minutes until fragrant, being careful not to burn it.

3. Pour in the dry white wine, scraping the bottom of the pan to release any flavorful bits. Allow the wine to simmer for 2-3 minutes, letting the alcohol evaporate.

4. Add the cleaned Penn Cove clams to the pan, stirring gently to coat them with the flavorful mixture. Cover the pan with a lid and let the clams steam for 8-10 minutes or until they open. Discard any clams that do not open.

5. Toss in the halved cherry tomatoes and fresh parsley, stirring to combine. Season with salt and black pepper to taste, and add red pepper flakes if you desire a touch of heat.

6. Serve the Penn Cove Clams with House Pancetta in shallow bowls, accompanied by crusty bread to soak up the savory broth.

Nutrition Information:
(Per serving)
- Calories: 380
- Protein: 20g
- Fat: 18g
- Carbohydrates: 20g
- Fiber: 2g
- Sugar: 2g
- Sodium: 850mg

Immerse yourself in the flavors of the Pacific with this delightful dish—a testament to the culinary artistry that defines the menu at Tom Douglas's Serious Pie restaurant.

9. Soft Farm Egg, House Pancetta & Arugula

Indulge in the culinary symphony inspired by the iconic Serious Pie restaurant with our rendition of "Soft Farm Egg, House Pancetta & Arugula." This dish captures the essence of Tom Douglas's renowned establishment, offering a harmonious blend of textures and flavors. The marriage of velvety farm-fresh eggs, crispy house-made pancetta, and the peppery bite of arugula creates a breakfast masterpiece that's simple yet sophisticated. Elevate your brunch experience with this exquisite dish that pays homage to Serious Pie's commitment to quality and creativity.

Serving: 4 servings
Preparation Time: 15 minutes
Ready Time: 30 minutes

Ingredients:
- 4 farm-fresh eggs
- 8 slices of house-made pancetta
- 2 cups fresh arugula, washed and dried
- 2 tablespoons olive oil
- Salt and black pepper to taste

Instructions:
1. Preheat the Oven:
Preheat your oven to 375°F (190°C).
2. Prepare the Pancetta:
Lay the slices of house-made pancetta on a baking sheet lined with parchment paper. Bake in the preheated oven for 10-12 minutes or until the pancetta becomes crispy. Remove from the oven and set aside.
3. Soft-Boil the Eggs:
Fill a saucepan with water and bring it to a gentle boil. Carefully add the farm-fresh eggs to the boiling water and cook for 6 minutes. Transfer the eggs to a bowl of ice water to stop the cooking process. Once cooled, carefully peel the eggs and set them aside.
4. Sauté the Arugula:
In a skillet, heat olive oil over medium heat. Add the arugula and sauté for 2-3 minutes until it wilts slightly. Season with salt and black pepper to taste.
5. Assemble the Dish:
Place a bed of sautéed arugula on each plate. Gently cut each soft-boiled egg in half and arrange them on top of the arugula. Crumble the crispy pancetta over the eggs.
6. Finish and Serve:
Drizzle a little extra olive oil over the dish and sprinkle with additional black pepper if desired. Serve immediately, allowing the runny egg yolk to mingle with the arugula and pancetta for a delightful burst of flavors.

Nutrition Information:
(Per Serving)
- Calories: 320
- Protein: 18g
- Fat: 25g
- Carbohydrates: 3g
- Fiber: 1g
- Sugar: 0g
- Sodium: 600mg
Note: Nutrition information is approximate and may vary based on specific ingredients used.

10. Smoked Provolone with House Tomato Sauce

Indulge your taste buds in the smoky symphony of flavors with our delectable recipe for "Smoked Provolone with House Tomato Sauce." Inspired by the culinary masterpieces at Tom Douglas's Serious Pie restaurant, this dish elevates the classic combination of smoked provolone and rich tomato sauce to new heights. Perfect for a cozy night in or a gathering with friends, this recipe promises to transport you to the heart of Serious Pie's kitchen.

Serving: 4 servings
Preparation Time: 15 minutes
Ready Time: 30 minutes

Ingredients:
- 1 lb smoked provolone, sliced
- 2 cups house tomato sauce (recipe below)
- 1 tablespoon olive oil
- 2 cloves garlic, minced
- 1 teaspoon dried oregano
- Salt and pepper to taste
- Fresh basil leaves for garnish
House Tomato Sauce:
- 2 tablespoons olive oil
- 1 onion, finely chopped
- 2 cloves garlic, minced

- 1 can (28 oz) crushed tomatoes
- 1 teaspoon dried oregano
- 1 teaspoon sugar
- Salt and pepper to taste

Instructions:
House Tomato Sauce:
1. In a saucepan, heat olive oil over medium heat.
2. Add chopped onion and garlic, sauté until softened.
3. Pour in crushed tomatoes and add oregano, sugar, salt, and pepper.
4. Simmer over low heat for 20-25 minutes, stirring occasionally.
Smoked Provolone with House Tomato Sauce:
1. Preheat your oven to 375°F (190°C).
2. In a skillet, heat olive oil over medium heat. Add minced garlic and sauté until fragrant.
3. Pour in the house tomato sauce, add dried oregano, and season with salt and pepper to taste. Simmer for 5 minutes.
4. In a baking dish, layer the sliced smoked provolone.
5. Pour the warm house tomato sauce over the provolone, ensuring an even distribution.
6. Bake in the preheated oven for 15-20 minutes or until the cheese is melted and bubbly.
7. Garnish with fresh basil leaves just before serving.

Nutrition Information (per serving):
- Calories: 350
- Fat: 25g
- Saturated Fat: 12g
- Cholesterol: 50mg
- Sodium: 800mg
- Carbohydrates: 10g
- Fiber: 3g
- Sugar: 6g
- Protein: 20g
Indulge in the rich, smoky goodness of this Smoked Provolone with House Tomato Sauce—a dish that captures the essence of Serious Pie's culinary expertise in the comfort of your own home. Enjoy!

11. Guanciale, Soft Farm Egg & Pecorino

Indulge in the rustic charm of Italian flavors with our homage to Tom Douglas's Serious Pie restaurant – the exquisite "Guanciale, Soft Farm Egg & Pecorino." This dish combines the richness of guanciale, the creaminess of a soft farm egg, and the robust taste of Pecorino cheese, creating a symphony of textures and tastes that will transport you straight to the heart of Italy.

Serving: 2 servings
Preparation Time: 15 minutes
Ready Time: 25 minutes

Ingredients:
- 150g guanciale, thinly sliced
- 4 large farm-fresh eggs
- 150g Pecorino cheese, grated
- Freshly ground black pepper, to taste
- 1 tablespoon olive oil
- 1 teaspoon red pepper flakes (optional, for a hint of heat)
- Fresh parsley, chopped, for garnish

Instructions:
1. Preheat Oven:
Preheat your oven to 375°F (190°C).
2. Cook Guanciale:
In a skillet over medium heat, add the olive oil. Add the guanciale slices and cook until they become golden and crispy, about 5 minutes. Remove from the heat and set aside.
3. Prepare Eggs:
Carefully crack the farm-fresh eggs into individual small bowls.
4. Soft Boil Eggs:
In a saucepan, bring water to a gentle boil. Carefully lower the eggs into the water and cook for exactly 6 minutes. Remove the eggs and place them in an ice bath to stop the cooking process. Once cooled, gently peel the eggs.
5. Assemble:
Place a portion of the crispy guanciale on each plate. Top with a soft-boiled egg. Sprinkle Pecorino cheese generously over the egg, allowing the heat from the guanciale to slightly melt the cheese.

6. Season:
Grind black pepper over the dish, and if you desire a touch of heat, sprinkle red pepper flakes.
7. Garnish:
Finish with a sprinkle of fresh parsley for a burst of color and freshness.
8. Serve:
Serve immediately, allowing the soft egg yolk to mingle with the salty guanciale and rich Pecorino.

Nutrition Information:
(Per Serving)
- Calories: 450
- Protein: 22g
- Fat: 35g
- Carbohydrates: 2g
- Fiber: 0g
- Sugar: 0g
- Sodium: 800mg

Embrace the essence of Italian cuisine with this delightful amalgamation of guanciale, soft farm eggs, and Pecorino. A dish that exemplifies simplicity and sophistication on your plate, inspired by the culinary genius of Tom Douglas's Serious Pie restaurant.

12. Sweet Fennel Sausage with Roasted Pepper

Indulge your taste buds in the savory symphony of flavors inspired by Tom Douglas's Serious Pie restaurant. Our Sweet Fennel Sausage with Roasted Pepper is a culinary masterpiece that combines the aromatic essence of fennel-infused sausage with the smoky sweetness of roasted peppers. This dish pays homage to the innovative and mouthwatering creations that Serious Pie is celebrated for. Get ready to elevate your home cooking experience with this delectable recipe!

Serving: 4 servings
Preparation Time: 15 minutes
Ready Time: 45 minutes

Ingredients:

- 1 lb sweet fennel sausage, casings removed
- 2 red bell peppers, sliced into strips
- 1 yellow bell pepper, sliced into strips
- 1 tablespoon olive oil
- 1 teaspoon dried oregano
- 1 teaspoon garlic powder
- Salt and pepper to taste
- Fresh basil leaves for garnish (optional)

Instructions:
1. Preheat the oven to 400°F (200°C).
2. In a large mixing bowl, combine the sweet fennel sausage meat with dried oregano, garlic powder, salt, and pepper. Mix well until the seasonings are evenly distributed.
3. Form the seasoned sausage meat into small patties or meatballs, ensuring they are of uniform size for even cooking.
4. Heat olive oil in an oven-safe skillet over medium-high heat. Once hot, add the sausage patties and cook until browned on both sides, about 3-4 minutes per side. Remove the sausage from the skillet and set aside.
5. In the same skillet, add the sliced red and yellow bell peppers. Sauté until they begin to soften, about 3-5 minutes.
6. Return the browned sausage patties to the skillet, nestling them among the peppers.
7. Transfer the skillet to the preheated oven and roast for 20-25 minutes or until the sausage is cooked through and the peppers are tender.
8. Garnish with fresh basil leaves if desired and serve hot.

Nutrition Information:
(Per Serving)
- Calories: 380 kcal
- Protein: 18g
- Fat: 28g
- Carbohydrates: 10g
- Fiber: 2g
- Sugar: 5g
- Sodium: 800mg

Embrace the spirit of Serious Pie in your kitchen with this Sweet Fennel Sausage with Roasted Pepper recipe. Whether you're hosting a dinner party or enjoying a cozy night in, this dish is sure to impress with its harmonious blend of flavors.

13. Soft Farm Egg, Prosciutto & Red Onion

Indulge your palate in the exquisite flavors of Serious Pie, as we bring you a delightful recipe inspired by Tom Douglas's renowned restaurant. The Soft Farm Egg, Prosciutto & Red Onion dish is a harmonious blend of rich, velvety farm-fresh eggs, the savory allure of prosciutto, and the sweet crunch of red onions. Elevate your culinary experience with this sophisticated yet simple creation that pays homage to the culinary artistry of Serious Pie.

Serving: 4 servings
Preparation Time: 15 minutes
Ready Time: 20 minutes

Ingredients:
- 4 farm-fresh eggs
- 4 slices of prosciutto
- 1 medium-sized red onion, thinly sliced
- 2 tablespoons olive oil
- Salt and pepper to taste
- Fresh chives for garnish

Instructions:
1. Prepare the Ingredients:
- Crack the eggs into separate bowls, ensuring not to break the yolks.
- Thinly slice the red onion.
- Lay out the prosciutto slices.
2. Preheat the Oven:
- Preheat your oven to 375°F (190°C).
3. Sauté the Red Onions:
- In a skillet, heat 1 tablespoon of olive oil over medium heat.
- Add the sliced red onions and sauté until they become caramelized and slightly golden. Set aside.
4. Prepare the Prosciutto:
- On a baking sheet, arrange the prosciutto slices. Bake in the preheated oven for 5-7 minutes or until the edges become crispy. Remove from the oven and set aside.

5. Soft Farm Eggs:
- In a separate non-stick pan, add the remaining olive oil and heat over medium-low heat.
- Carefully slide the eggs into the pan, ensuring not to break the yolks.
- Cook until the whites are set but the yolks remain runny.
6. Assemble the Dish:
- Place a spoonful of sautéed red onions on each plate.
- Gently transfer a soft farm egg onto the bed of red onions.
- Drape a slice of crispy prosciutto over each egg.
- Season with salt and pepper to taste.
7. Garnish and Serve:
- Sprinkle fresh chives over the dish for a burst of color and added freshness.
- Serve immediately, allowing the warmth of the eggs to complement the crispiness of the prosciutto and the sweetness of the red onions.

Nutrition Information (per serving):
- Calories: 240
- Protein: 12g
- Fat: 18g
- Carbohydrates: 5g
- Fiber: 1g
- Sugar: 2g
- Sodium: 600mg
Indulge in this Soft Farm Egg, Prosciutto & Red Onion creation inspired by the culinary genius of Serious Pie. A perfect blend of textures and flavors awaits you, capturing the essence of Tom Douglas's iconic restaurant in the comfort of your home.

14. Truffle Cheese with Soft Farm Egg

Indulge in the exquisite flavors of Tom Douglas's Serious Pie restaurant with our delectable recipe for Truffle Cheese with Soft Farm Egg. This sophisticated dish combines the earthy richness of truffle-infused cheese with the velvety texture of a soft farm egg, creating a symphony of flavors that is both comforting and luxurious. Elevate your culinary experience with this inspired creation that mirrors the exceptional offerings of one of Seattle's finest establishments.

Serving: 2 servings
Preparation Time: 15 minutes
Ready Time: 20 minutes

Ingredients:
- 4 large farm-fresh eggs
- 1 cup truffle-infused cheese, shaved (choose your favorite variety)
- 1 tablespoon truffle oil
- 1 tablespoon unsalted butter
- Salt and black pepper to taste
- Fresh chives, finely chopped, for garnish (optional)

Instructions:
1. Preheat the Oven:
Preheat your oven to 375°F (190°C).
2. Prepare Ramekins:
Lightly butter two individual-sized ramekins. Crack two eggs into each ramekin, ensuring the yolks remain intact.
3. Cheese Layer:
Sprinkle the shaved truffle cheese evenly over the eggs in each ramekin.
4. Truffle Infusion:
Drizzle a half tablespoon of truffle oil over each egg and cheese combination. Season with a pinch of salt and black pepper to enhance the flavors.
5. Bake to Perfection:
Place the ramekins in the preheated oven and bake for approximately 12-15 minutes or until the egg whites are set, but the yolks remain runny.
6. Final Touch:
Carefully remove the ramekins from the oven. Add a small knob of butter on top of each egg, allowing it to melt and enrich the dish. Garnish with fresh chives if desired.
7. Serve Warm:
Serve immediately, allowing the diners to savor the luxurious combination of truffle-infused cheese and the luscious soft farm eggs.

Nutrition Information:
Note: Nutritional values are approximate and may vary based on specific ingredients used.
- Calories per serving: 350

- Protein: 18g
- Fat: 28g
- Carbohydrates: 2g
- Fiber: 0g
- Sugar: 0g
- Cholesterol: 420mg
- Sodium: 600mg

Elevate your home cooking experience with this decadent Truffle Cheese with Soft Farm Egg recipe inspired by the culinary mastery of Tom Douglas's Serious Pie.

15. Hazelnut Brown Butter Cake

Indulge your senses in the rich, nutty decadence of our Hazelnut Brown Butter Cake, a delectable creation inspired by the menu of Tom Douglas's renowned Serious Pie restaurant. This dessert masterpiece perfectly captures the essence of Serious Pie's commitment to bold flavors and impeccable craftsmanship. Elevate your culinary experience with this irresistible Hazelnut Brown Butter Cake that marries the deep, toasty notes of hazelnuts with the luxurious essence of brown butter. Whether you're a seasoned baker or a kitchen enthusiast, this dessert is sure to become a standout favorite.

Serving: Serves 8-10
Preparation Time: 20 minutes
Ready Time: 1 hour 30 minutes

Ingredients:
- 1 cup unsalted butter
- 1 cup all-purpose flour
- 1 cup hazelnuts, finely ground
- 1 cup granulated sugar
- 1/2 cup brown sugar, packed
- 4 large eggs
- 1 teaspoon vanilla extract
- 1/2 teaspoon baking powder
- 1/4 teaspoon salt
- Powdered sugar (for dusting, optional)

Instructions:
1. Preheat Oven:
Preheat your oven to 350°F (175°C). Grease and flour a 9-inch round cake pan.
2. Brown the Butter:
In a saucepan over medium heat, melt the butter. Continue to cook, stirring frequently, until the butter turns golden brown and has a nutty aroma. Be cautious not to burn it. Remove from heat and let it cool slightly.
3. Combine Dry Ingredients:
In a bowl, whisk together the all-purpose flour, ground hazelnuts, baking powder, and salt.
4. Beat Sugars and Eggs:
In a large mixing bowl, beat together the granulated sugar, brown sugar, and eggs until the mixture is pale and fluffy.
5. Add Vanilla and Brown Butter:
Stir in the vanilla extract and gradually add the brown butter, mixing until well combined.
6. Incorporate Dry Ingredients:
Gently fold in the dry ingredients until the batter is smooth and well incorporated.
7. Bake:
Pour the batter into the prepared cake pan and smooth the top. Bake in the preheated oven for 40-45 minutes or until a toothpick inserted into the center comes out clean.
8. Cool and Serve:
Allow the cake to cool in the pan for 15 minutes before transferring it to a wire rack to cool completely. Dust with powdered sugar if desired. Slice and serve.

Nutrition Information:
(Per Serving)
- Calories: 380
- Total Fat: 26g
- Saturated Fat: 12g
- Trans Fat: 0g
- Cholesterol: 125mg
- Sodium: 90mg
- Total Carbohydrates: 32g

- Dietary Fiber: 2g
- Sugars: 20g
- Protein: 6g
Note: Nutrition information is approximate and may vary based on specific ingredients used.

16. Penn Cove Clams with Chili Flakes

Indulge in the tantalizing flavors of the Pacific Northwest with this exquisite recipe inspired by Tom Douglas's Serious Pie restaurant. The Penn Cove Clams with Chili Flakes showcase the region's finest seafood, paired with a subtle kick of spice to elevate your taste buds. This dish embodies the culinary excellence of Serious Pie, offering a delightful blend of freshness and heat that will leave you craving more.

Serving: 4 servings
Preparation Time: 15 minutes
Ready Time: 30 minutes

Ingredients:
- 2 pounds fresh Penn Cove clams, scrubbed and cleaned
- 2 tablespoons olive oil
- 4 cloves garlic, minced
- 1 teaspoon red chili flakes (adjust to taste)
- 1 cup dry white wine
- 1/4 cup fresh parsley, chopped
- Salt and black pepper to taste
- Crusty bread for serving

Instructions:
1. In a large, deep skillet, heat olive oil over medium heat.
2. Add minced garlic and red chili flakes, sautéing until garlic becomes fragrant, but be cautious not to brown.
3. Gently place the cleaned clams into the skillet, stirring to coat them with the garlic and chili-infused oil.
4. Pour in the white wine, cover the skillet, and allow the clams to steam for 5-7 minutes or until they open. Discard any clams that do not open.

5. Season with salt and black pepper to taste. Toss in chopped parsley and stir to combine.
6. Serve the Penn Cove Clams in individual bowls, accompanied by slices of crusty bread for soaking up the delicious broth.

Nutrition Information:
Note: Nutritional values may vary based on specific ingredients used and portion sizes.
- Calories: 250 per serving
- Protein: 22g
- Fat: 10g
- Carbohydrates: 12g
- Fiber: 1g
- Sugar: 1g
- Sodium: 600mg
Savor the rich flavors of the Pacific with this Tom Douglas-inspired recipe, where the freshness of Penn Cove clams meets the bold warmth of chili flakes. Perfect for a cozy dinner or entertaining guests, this dish captures the essence of Serious Pie's culinary expertise.

17. Finocchiona Salami, Castelvetrano Olives & Tomato

This recipe pays homage to the delectable flavors found at Tom Douglas's Serious Pie restaurant. The combination of savory Finocchiona salami, briny Castelvetrano olives, and ripe tomatoes creates a tantalizing dish that showcases the essence of Italian cuisine.

Serving: 2 servings
Preparation time: 10 minutes
Ready time: 10 minutes

Ingredients:
- 6-8 slices of Finocchiona salami
- 1 cup Castelvetrano olives, pitted and halved
- 2 ripe tomatoes, sliced
- 2 tablespoons extra-virgin olive oil
- 1 tablespoon balsamic vinegar

- Fresh basil leaves, for garnish
- Salt and pepper to taste

Instructions:
1. Arrange the slices of Finocchiona salami on a serving platter.
2. Scatter the halved Castelvetrano olives over the salami slices.
3. Place the tomato slices on top of the salami and olives.
4. In a small bowl, whisk together the extra-virgin olive oil and balsamic vinegar. Drizzle this dressing over the tomatoes.
5. Season with salt and pepper to taste.
6. Garnish the dish with fresh basil leaves.
7. Serve immediately and enjoy the vibrant flavors.

Nutrition Information: (per serving)
- Calories: Approximately 250 kcal
- Total Fat: 20g
- Saturated Fat: 4g
- Cholesterol: 20mg
- Sodium: 700mg
- Total Carbohydrates: 10g
- Dietary Fiber: 4g
- Sugars: 4g
- Protein: 10g
Note: Nutrition Information is approximate and may vary based on specific ingredients used.
This dish offers a quick and easy way to savor the delightful tastes of Serious Pie's menu in the comfort of your own home. Enjoy the harmonious blend of flavors that come together beautifully in this Finocchiona Salami, Castelvetrano Olives & Tomato recipe!

18. Buffalo Mozzarella, San Marzano Tomato & Basil

This delightful dish of Buffalo Mozzarella, San Marzano Tomato & Basil is a culinary masterpiece inspired by the menu at Tom Douglas's Serious Pie restaurant. Bursting with freshness and flavors reminiscent of Italian cuisine, this dish combines the creaminess of buffalo mozzarella, the vibrant sweetness of San Marzano tomatoes, and the aromatic touch of basil, creating a symphony of taste on the palate.

Serving: 2-4 servings
Preparation time: 15 minutes
Ready time: 15 minutes

Ingredients:
- 2 large San Marzano tomatoes, thinly sliced
- 8 ounces Buffalo mozzarella, sliced
- 1 bunch fresh basil leaves
- Extra virgin olive oil
- Balsamic glaze (optional)
- Sea salt and freshly ground black pepper to taste

Instructions:
1. Preparation:
- Preheat your oven to 375°F (190°C).
- Slice the San Marzano tomatoes and buffalo mozzarella into thin rounds.
2. Assembling the Dish:
- On a baking sheet, arrange the sliced San Marzano tomatoes and buffalo mozzarella alternately, slightly overlapping each other.
3. Adding Basil and Seasoning:
- Place fresh basil leaves between the tomato and mozzarella slices.
- Drizzle a generous amount of extra virgin olive oil over the assembled dish.
- Sprinkle with sea salt and freshly ground black pepper according to taste.
4. Baking:
- Place the baking sheet in the preheated oven and bake for about 10-12 minutes or until the cheese starts to melt and the tomatoes are tender.
5. Final Touch (Optional):
- If desired, once out of the oven, lightly drizzle balsamic glaze over the dish for an extra burst of flavor.
6. Serve:
- Carefully transfer the warm Buffalo Mozzarella, San Marzano Tomato & Basil onto a serving platter.
- Garnish with a few additional fresh basil leaves for a vibrant touch.
- Serve immediately and enjoy this exquisite dish.

Nutrition Information (approximate values per serving):
- Calories: 220 kcal
- Total Fat: 16g
- Saturated Fat: 9g
- Cholesterol: 45mg
- Sodium: 380mg
- Total Carbohydrate: 5g
- Dietary Fiber: 2g
- Sugars: 3g
- Protein: 14g

(Nutrition information may vary depending on specific ingredients and portion sizes used.)

This Buffalo Mozzarella, San Marzano Tomato & Basil dish is a harmonious blend of simplicity and sophistication, reflecting the authentic flavors found in Tom Douglas's Serious Pie restaurant. Enjoy this appetizing creation as a starter or as a delightful accompaniment to your favorite meal.

19. Wild Mushrooms with Truffle Cheese

'Tom Douglas's Serious Pie restaurant is renowned for its innovative and delectable dishes, where flavors converge to create unforgettable culinary experiences. One such dish, 'Wild Mushrooms with Truffle Cheese,' combines the earthy richness of wild mushrooms with the luxurious essence of truffle cheese. This recipe celebrates the robust flavors found in nature and elevates them with the indulgence of truffle-infused cheese, delivering a gastronomic delight that's both sophisticated and comforting."

Serving: Serves 4
Preparation Time: 20 minutes
Ready Time: 40 minutes

Ingredients:
- 1 pound mixed wild mushrooms (such as chanterelles, shiitake, oyster)
- 2 tablespoons olive oil
- 2 cloves garlic, minced

- Salt and pepper to taste
- 1 tablespoon fresh thyme leaves
- 4 ounces truffle cheese, grated or thinly sliced
- 1 pre-made pizza dough (store-bought or homemade)

Instructions:
1. Preheat the oven to the temperature specified on the pizza dough package or to 450°F (230°C).
2. Clean the wild mushrooms thoroughly and slice them into bite-sized pieces if they are large.
3. Heat the olive oil in a skillet over medium-high heat. Add the minced garlic and sauté for about 30 seconds until fragrant.
4. Add the sliced mushrooms to the skillet and cook, stirring occasionally, until they release their moisture and start to brown, about 8-10 minutes. Season with salt, pepper, and fresh thyme leaves. Remove from heat and set aside.
5. Roll out the pizza dough on a floured surface into your desired shape and thickness.
6. Transfer the rolled-out dough to a baking sheet or pizza stone.
7. Spread the cooked mushrooms evenly over the dough, leaving a small border around the edges.
8. Distribute the grated or thinly sliced truffle cheese over the mushrooms.
9. Place the baking sheet or pizza stone in the preheated oven and bake for 12-15 minutes or until the crust is golden brown and the cheese is melted and bubbly.
10. Remove the pizza from the oven and let it cool for a few minutes before slicing.
11. Serve the Wild Mushrooms with Truffle Cheese pizza hot, garnished with additional fresh thyme if desired.

Nutrition Information:
(Note: Nutrition information may vary based on specific ingredients and portion sizes used. Below values are approximate.)
- Calories: 350 per serving
- Total Fat: 15g
- Saturated Fat: 6g
- Cholesterol: 15mg
- Sodium: 500mg
- Total Carbohydrates: 40g

- Dietary Fiber: 3g
- Sugars: 2g
- Protein: 12g

Enjoy the rich, earthy flavors of this exquisite pizza, perfect for a cozy evening or as a showstopping appetizer for guests!

20. Soft Farm Egg, Prosciutto, Arugula & Pecorino

Indulge in the culinary artistry inspired by Tom Douglas's Serious Pie restaurant with this exquisite dish featuring soft farm eggs, savory prosciutto, peppery arugula, and the distinct flavor of Pecorino cheese. This recipe perfectly captures the essence of Serious Pie's commitment to quality ingredients and innovative combinations. Elevate your brunch or light dinner with the harmonious blend of textures and flavors in this Soft Farm Egg, Prosciutto, Arugula & Pecorino creation.

Serving: 4 servings
Preparation Time: 15 minutes
Ready Time: 20 minutes

Ingredients:
- 4 farm-fresh eggs
- 4 slices of prosciutto
- 2 cups fresh arugula
- 1/2 cup shaved Pecorino cheese
- Salt and pepper to taste
- Olive oil for drizzling

Instructions:
1. Preheat the Oven:
- Preheat your oven to 375°F (190°C).
2. Prepare the Eggs:
- Carefully crack each egg into a small bowl, ensuring not to break the yolk.
3. Bake the Eggs:
- Place the eggs in individual ramekins or oven-safe dishes.
- Bake in the preheated oven for 12-15 minutes or until the whites are set, but the yolks remain soft.

4. Crisp the Prosciutto:
- In a skillet over medium heat, lightly crisp the prosciutto slices for about 2 minutes per side. Set aside.
5. Assemble the Dish:
- Divide the arugula among four plates, creating a bed for the eggs.
- Gently place a baked egg on top of the arugula on each plate.
- Drape a slice of crisp prosciutto over each egg.
- Sprinkle shaved Pecorino cheese over the entire dish.
- Season with salt and pepper to taste.
6. Drizzle with Olive Oil:
- Finish the dish by drizzling a bit of high-quality olive oil over each serving.
7. Serve:
- Serve immediately, allowing the warmth of the eggs to slightly wilt the arugula.

Nutrition Information:
- *Note: Nutrition information may vary based on specific ingredients used.*
- Calories per serving: XXX
- Protein: XXXg
- Fat: XXXg
- Carbohydrates: XXXg
- Fiber: XXXg
Indulge in the luxurious simplicity of this Soft Farm Egg, Prosciutto, Arugula & Pecorino dish – a testament to the inspired culinary creations found at Tom Douglas's Serious Pie restaurant.

21. Sweet Fennel Sausage with Roasted Red Pepper

Indulge your taste buds in the exquisite flavors inspired by Tom Douglas's Serious Pie restaurant with this delectable Sweet Fennel Sausage with Roasted Red Pepper recipe. The combination of succulent sweet fennel sausage and smoky roasted red pepper creates a symphony of taste that mirrors the culinary expertise found in Serious Pie's menu. Elevate your home cooking experience with this savory delight that captures the essence of Tom Douglas's renowned culinary creations.

Serving: 4 servings
Preparation Time: 15 minutes
Ready Time: 45 minutes

Ingredients:
- 1 pound sweet fennel sausage links
- 2 large red bell peppers, roasted and sliced
- 2 tablespoons olive oil
- 1 teaspoon fennel seeds
- 1 teaspoon smoked paprika
- Salt and black pepper to taste
- Fresh parsley, chopped (for garnish)

Instructions:
1. Preheat the Oven:
- Preheat your oven to 400°F (200°C).
2. Roast the Red Peppers:
- Place the whole red bell peppers on a baking sheet.
- Roast in the preheated oven for 25-30 minutes, turning occasionally until the skin is charred and blistered.
- Remove from the oven and place the roasted peppers in a bowl, covering with plastic wrap. Let them cool, then peel, seed, and slice into thin strips.
3. Cook the Sausages:
- Heat olive oil in a large oven-safe skillet over medium heat.
- Add sweet fennel sausages to the skillet and cook until browned on all sides, about 8-10 minutes.
4. Add Flavors:
- Sprinkle fennel seeds and smoked paprika over the sausages.
- Season with salt and black pepper to taste.
5. Combine with Roasted Red Peppers:
- Add the roasted red pepper strips to the skillet, mixing them with the sausages.
6. Finish in the Oven:
- Transfer the skillet to the preheated oven and bake for an additional 15-20 minutes until the sausages are cooked through.
7. Garnish and Serve:
- Sprinkle the dish with chopped fresh parsley before serving.

Nutrition Information:

Note: Nutrition information is approximate and may vary based on specific ingredients and portion sizes.
- Calories per serving: 400 kcal
- Protein: 18g
- Carbohydrates: 6g
- Fat: 34g
- Saturated Fat: 10g
- Cholesterol: 70mg
- Sodium: 800mg
- Fiber: 2g
- Sugar: 3g

Embrace the robust flavors of Serious Pie's culinary magic in your own kitchen with this Sweet Fennel Sausage with Roasted Red Pepper recipe. Perfect for a cozy dinner or a gathering with friends, this dish is a testament to the rich and diverse tastes celebrated at Tom Douglas's acclaimed restaurant.

22. Anchovy & Soft Farm Egg with Tomato Sauce

Elevate your taste buds with this exquisite Anchovy & Soft Farm Egg with Tomato Sauce inspired by the culinary wonders of Tom Douglas's Serious Pie restaurant. This dish is a harmonious blend of rich umami flavors from anchovies, the creaminess of soft farm-fresh eggs, and the vibrant essence of a luscious tomato sauce. Prepare to embark on a gastronomic journey that captures the essence of Serious Pie's innovative menu.

Serving: 4 servings
Preparation Time: 15 minutes
Ready Time: 30 minutes

Ingredients:
- 4 large farm eggs
- 2 tablespoons olive oil
- 1 small red onion, finely chopped
- 2 cloves garlic, minced
- 1 can (14 ounces) crushed tomatoes
- 8-10 anchovy fillets, finely chopped

- 1 teaspoon red pepper flakes (adjust to taste)
- Salt and black pepper to taste
- 1 tablespoon fresh parsley, chopped (for garnish)

Instructions:
1. Prepare Tomato Sauce:
- In a medium-sized saucepan, heat olive oil over medium heat.
- Add finely chopped red onion and sauté until softened, about 3-4 minutes.
- Add minced garlic and sauté for an additional 1-2 minutes until fragrant.
- Pour in crushed tomatoes, chopped anchovies, red pepper flakes, salt, and black pepper.
- Simmer the sauce over medium-low heat for 15-20 minutes, allowing the flavors to meld and the sauce to thicken. Stir occasionally.
2. Soft Farm Eggs:
- While the tomato sauce simmers, prepare the soft farm eggs.
- Bring a medium-sized pot of water to a gentle simmer.
- Crack each egg into a small bowl.
- Create a gentle whirlpool in the simmering water and carefully slide each egg into the center.
- Poach the eggs for about 3-4 minutes until the whites are set but the yolks remain runny. Remove with a slotted spoon.
3. Assembly:
- Place a generous spoonful of the tomato sauce on each plate.
- Gently nestle a soft farm egg on top of the sauce.
- Drizzle with additional tomato sauce and sprinkle with fresh parsley.
4. Serve:
- Serve immediately, allowing the rich, runny yolk to mingle with the savory tomato sauce.

Nutrition Information (per serving):
(Note: Nutritional values may vary based on specific ingredients and portion sizes. The values provided are approximate.)
- Calories: 220
- Protein: 12g
- Fat: 15g
- Carbohydrates: 10g
- Fiber: 3g
- Sugar: 5g

- Sodium: 800mg

Indulge in the bold and savory flavors of this Anchovy & Soft Farm Egg with Tomato Sauce—a culinary masterpiece inspired by the brilliance of Tom Douglas's Serious Pie.

23. Roasted Chanterelle Mushrooms with Truffle Cheese

Indulge your taste buds in the exquisite flavors inspired by Tom Douglas's Serious Pie restaurant with our Roasted Chanterelle Mushrooms with Truffle Cheese recipe. This dish combines the earthy richness of chanterelle mushrooms with the luxurious essence of truffle cheese, creating a culinary experience that's both sophisticated and comforting.

Serving: 4 servings
Preparation Time: 15 minutes
Ready Time: 30 minutes

Ingredients:
- 1 pound fresh chanterelle mushrooms, cleaned and trimmed
- 2 tablespoons olive oil
- Salt and pepper to taste
- 1 cup truffle cheese, shaved or grated
- 2 tablespoons fresh thyme leaves, chopped
- 2 cloves garlic, minced
- 1 tablespoon balsamic glaze (optional, for drizzling)

Instructions:
1. Preheat the Oven:
- Preheat your oven to 400°F (200°C).
2. Prepare the Chanterelle Mushrooms:
- Place the cleaned and trimmed chanterelle mushrooms on a baking sheet.
3. Season the Mushrooms:
- Drizzle the mushrooms with olive oil, ensuring they are well-coated. Sprinkle with salt and pepper to taste.
4. Roast the Mushrooms:

- Roast the mushrooms in the preheated oven for 15-20 minutes or until they are golden brown and tender, stirring halfway through for even cooking.

5. Add Garlic and Thyme:
- In the last 5 minutes of roasting, add minced garlic and chopped thyme to the mushrooms, tossing to combine. This enhances the flavors and aromas.

6. Serve with Truffle Cheese:
- Once roasted, transfer the mushrooms to a serving platter and generously sprinkle shaved or grated truffle cheese over the top. The residual heat will melt the cheese slightly.

7. Drizzle with Balsamic Glaze (Optional):
- For an extra layer of flavor, drizzle the dish with balsamic glaze before serving.

8. Garnish and Serve:
- Garnish with additional thyme leaves if desired. Serve the Roasted Chanterelle Mushrooms with Truffle Cheese as a side dish or a luxurious appetizer.

Nutrition Information:
- *Note: Nutritional values may vary based on specific ingredients and quantities used.*
- Calories: XXX per serving
- Protein: XXX g
- Carbohydrates: XXX g
- Fat: XXX g
- Fiber: XXX g
- Sodium: XXX mg

Elevate your dining experience with this Tom Douglas-inspired creation, where the delicate flavors of chanterelle mushrooms meet the decadence of truffle cheese. A dish that's sure to leave a lasting impression!

24. Penn Cove Clams with House Pancetta & Lemon

Indulge your taste buds in a symphony of flavors with this exquisite recipe inspired by the renowned Serious Pie restaurant. Tom Douglas's culinary prowess shines through in every bite of these Penn Cove Clams with House Pancetta & Lemon. Elevate your dining experience with the rich combination of succulent clams, house-cured pancetta, and the zesty brightness of fresh lemon. This dish is a celebration of the Pacific Northwest's culinary treasures, inviting you to savor the ocean's bounty in the comfort of your home.

Serving: 4 servings
Preparation Time: 20 minutes
Ready Time: 30 minutes

Ingredients:
- 2 pounds Penn Cove clams, scrubbed and cleaned
- 1/2 pound house-cured pancetta, diced
- 2 tablespoons olive oil
- 1 small onion, finely chopped
- 4 cloves garlic, minced
- 1 cup dry white wine
- Zest of 1 lemon
- Juice of 1 lemon
- 1/4 cup fresh parsley, chopped
- Salt and pepper to taste

Instructions:
1. In a large skillet or deep pan, heat the olive oil over medium heat. Add the diced pancetta and sauté until golden brown and crispy.
2. Add the chopped onion to the pan and cook until softened, stirring occasionally. Add the minced garlic and continue to sauté for another minute until fragrant.
3. Pour in the dry white wine, scraping the bottom of the pan to release any flavorful bits. Allow the wine to simmer for 2-3 minutes.
4. Carefully add the cleaned Penn Cove clams to the pan, tossing them with the pancetta and aromatics. Cover the pan with a lid and let the clams steam for 5-7 minutes or until they open.
5. Once the clams have opened, stir in the lemon zest and juice. Season with salt and pepper to taste.
6. Sprinkle the chopped fresh parsley over the clams and give everything a gentle toss to combine.
7. Serve the Penn Cove Clams with House Pancetta & Lemon in deep bowls, ensuring to ladle the flavorful broth over the top.

Nutrition Information:
(Per serving)
- Calories: 320
- Protein: 20g
- Fat: 15g
- Carbohydrates: 15g
- Fiber: 2g
- Sugars: 2g
- Sodium: 800mg

Delight in the oceanic charm and robust flavors of Tom Douglas's Serious Pie with this tantalizing clam dish. Perfect for a cozy dinner or a gathering with friends, it's a taste of the Pacific Northwest on your plate.

25. Smoked Provolone, Tomato Sauce & Sweet Fennel Sausage

Indulge in the culinary delights inspired by Tom Douglas's Serious Pie restaurant with our flavorful "Smoked Provolone, Tomato Sauce & Sweet Fennel Sausage" pizza. This recipe captures the essence of Serious Pie's commitment to high-quality ingredients and innovative flavor combinations. The rich smokiness of Provolone, the tanginess of tomato sauce, and the savory sweetness of fennel sausage come together on a perfect pizza crust, creating a symphony of flavors that will transport you to the heart of Seattle's vibrant food scene.

Serving: 4 servings
Preparation Time: 20 minutes
Ready Time: 30 minutes

Ingredients:
- 1 pound pizza dough, store-bought or homemade
- 1 cup tomato sauce
- 2 cups smoked Provolone cheese, shredded
- 1 cup sweet fennel sausage, cooked and crumbled
- 1 tablespoon olive oil
- Fresh basil leaves for garnish (optional)

Instructions:

1. Preheat your oven to the highest temperature it can go (usually around 475-500°F or 245-260°C). If you have a pizza stone, place it in the oven to heat.
2. Roll out the pizza dough on a lightly floured surface to your desired thickness.
3. Transfer the rolled-out dough to a pizza peel or an inverted baking sheet dusted with cornmeal to prevent sticking.
4. Spread a generous layer of tomato sauce over the pizza dough, leaving a small border around the edges.
5. Evenly distribute the shredded smoked Provolone cheese over the tomato sauce.
6. Sprinkle the crumbled sweet fennel sausage over the cheese.
7. Drizzle olive oil over the pizza for added richness.
8. If using a pizza stone, carefully transfer the pizza to the preheated stone in the oven. If not using a stone, simply place the baking sheet with the pizza in the oven.
9. Bake for about 10-12 minutes or until the crust is golden and the cheese is bubbly and slightly browned.
10. Remove the pizza from the oven, and if desired, garnish with fresh basil leaves.
11. Allow the pizza to cool for a few minutes before slicing and serving.

Nutrition Information:
(Per Serving)
- Calories: 550
- Total Fat: 25g
- Saturated Fat: 10g
- Trans Fat: 0g
- Cholesterol: 50mg
- Sodium: 1200mg
- Total Carbohydrates: 55g
- Dietary Fiber: 3g
- Sugars: 4g
- Protein: 22g
Note: Nutrition information is approximate and may vary based on specific ingredients and portion sizes.

26. Prosciutto, Pecorino & Arugula with Olive Oil

This dish is a harmonious blend of bold flavors, drawing inspiration from the artisanal pizzas of Tom Douglas's Serious Pie restaurant. The saltiness of prosciutto, the sharpness of Pecorino cheese, and the peppery bite of arugula come together in perfect balance, elevated by the richness of olive oil.

Serving: Serves 2
Preparation Time: 10 minutes
Ready Time: 10 minutes

Ingredients:
- 6 slices of prosciutto
- 1 cup arugula, washed and dried
- 1/2 cup shaved Pecorino cheese
- 2 tablespoons extra-virgin olive oil

Instructions:
1. Lay out the prosciutto slices on a serving platter, creating a single layer.
2. Scatter the arugula evenly over the prosciutto slices.
3. Sprinkle the shaved Pecorino cheese over the arugula.
4. Drizzle the extra-virgin olive oil generously over the top of the ingredients.
5. Serve immediately and enjoy the delightful combination of flavors.

Nutrition Information:
Note: Nutritional values are approximate and may vary based on specific ingredients used.
- Calories: 250 per serving
- Total Fat: 20g
- Saturated Fat: 6g
- Trans Fat: 0g
- Cholesterol: 30mg
- Sodium: 650mg
- Total Carbohydrate: 1g
- Dietary Fiber: 0g
- Sugars: 0g
- Protein: 15g

This dish is a quick and elegant appetizer or light meal that celebrates the essence of Italian flavors. The simplicity of its preparation belies the complexity of taste it offers.

27. Guanciale, Castelvetrano Olives & Tomato Sauce

This recipe for Guanciale, Castelvetrano Olives & Tomato Sauce is a flavorful homage to the culinary delights served at Tom Douglas's Serious Pie restaurant. It combines the rich, savory flavors of guanciale, the briny goodness of Castelvetrano olives, and the tangy sweetness of tomato sauce to create a deliciously indulgent dish that's perfect for pasta or topping on crusty bread.

Serving: 4 servings
Preparation time: 15 minutes
Ready time: 45 minutes

Nutrition Information: *(per serving, approximate)*
Calories: 320
Total Fat: 22g
Saturated Fat: 6g
Cholesterol: 30mg
Sodium: 800mg
Total Carbohydrates: 20g
Dietary Fiber: 4g
Sugar: 8g
Protein: 10g

Ingredients:
- 8 ounces guanciale, diced
- 1 tablespoon olive oil
- 3 cloves garlic, minced
- 1 can (28 ounces) crushed tomatoes
- 1/2 cup Castelvetrano olives, pitted and chopped
- Salt and black pepper to taste
- Red pepper flakes (optional)
- Fresh basil leaves, torn, for garnish
- Grated Parmesan cheese, for serving (optional)

Instructions:
1. Heat olive oil in a large skillet over medium heat. Add diced guanciale and cook until it turns golden and releases its fat, about 5-7 minutes.
2. Add minced garlic to the skillet and sauté for an additional 1-2 minutes until fragrant.
3. Pour in the crushed tomatoes and bring the mixture to a gentle simmer. Reduce the heat to low and let it cook uncovered for 25-30 minutes, stirring occasionally, until the sauce thickens slightly.
4. Add the chopped Castelvetrano olives to the sauce, stirring to incorporate. Season with salt, black pepper, and red pepper flakes if desired. Simmer for another 5-10 minutes.
5. Taste and adjust seasoning if needed. Remove from heat.
6. Serve the sauce over your choice of pasta or as a topping on crusty bread. Garnish with torn fresh basil leaves and grated Parmesan cheese if desired.

This hearty and flavorful sauce will elevate any pasta dish or add a burst of flavor to your favorite bread. Enjoy the rich blend of guanciale, olives, and tomato sauce inspired by the culinary delights of Tom Douglas's Serious Pie restaurant!

28. Yukon Gold Potato, Rosemary & Caciocavallo

At Tom Douglas's Serious Pie, the Yukon Gold Potato, Rosemary & Caciocavallo pizza embodies a harmonious blend of flavors, showcasing the richness of Yukon Gold potatoes, the earthy essence of rosemary, and the delightful tang of Caciocavallo cheese. This recipe captures the essence of the restaurant's renowned pies, offering a savory delight that celebrates simplicity and quality ingredients.

Serving: Makes 1 pizza, approximately 10 inches in diameter.
Preparation Time: 15 minutes for dough preparation (if using store-bought dough)
15 minutes for ingredient preparation
Ready Time: 20-25 minutes baking time
Total: approximately 35-40 minutes

Ingredients:

- 1 ball of pizza dough (homemade or store-bought)
- 2 medium Yukon Gold potatoes, thinly sliced
- 1 tablespoon fresh rosemary, chopped
- 1 cup Caciocavallo cheese, grated
- 2 tablespoons olive oil
- Salt and freshly ground black pepper to taste
- Cornmeal or flour for dusting

Instructions:
1. Preheat your oven to 500°F (260°C) or as high as it can go, placing a pizza stone or baking sheet inside to heat up.
2. If using homemade dough, roll it out into a circle approximately 10 inches in diameter on a lightly floured surface. If using store-bought dough, allow it to come to room temperature and follow the package instructions.
3. Sprinkle cornmeal or flour on a pizza peel or an upside-down baking sheet to prevent sticking. Place the rolled-out dough on the prepared surface.
4. Drizzle a tablespoon of olive oil over the dough and spread it evenly with the back of a spoon.
5. Layer the thinly sliced Yukon Gold potatoes evenly over the dough, slightly overlapping them. Season with salt, black pepper, and chopped rosemary.
6. Sprinkle the grated Caciocavallo cheese generously over the potatoes.
7. Drizzle the remaining tablespoon of olive oil over the assembled pizza.
8. Carefully slide the pizza onto the preheated pizza stone or baking sheet in the oven. Bake for 20-25 minutes or until the crust is golden and the cheese is bubbly and lightly browned.
9. Once done, remove the pizza from the oven and let it cool for a few minutes before slicing. Garnish with additional fresh rosemary if desired.

Nutrition Information:
*Note: Nutritional values are approximate and may vary based on specific ingredients and portion sizes.
- Calories per serving: Approximately 320-350 calories
- Fat: Approximately 15-18g
- Carbohydrates: Approximately 35-40g
- Protein: Approximately 10-12g
Enjoy the savory delight of the Yukon Gold Potato, Rosemary & Caciocavallo pizza inspired by the flavors of Serious Pie!

29. Soft Farm Egg, Guanciale & Grana Padano

This dish, inspired by the innovative menu of Tom Douglas's Serious Pie restaurant, combines the velvety richness of a soft farm egg with the savory notes of crispy guanciale and the nutty depth of Grana Padano cheese. Each ingredient in this recipe harmonizes to create a symphony of flavors that exemplify the restaurant's commitment to quality ingredients and impeccable taste.

Serving: Serves 4
Preparation Time: 15 minutes
Ready Time: 25 minutes

Ingredients:
- 4 large farm-fresh eggs
- 4 slices of guanciale (Italian cured pork cheek)
- 1/2 cup grated Grana Padano cheese
- 1 tablespoon olive oil
- Freshly ground black pepper, to taste
- Chopped chives (optional, for garnish)

Instructions:
1. Preheat the Oven: Preheat your oven to 375°F (190°C).
2. Prepare the Guanciale: Place the guanciale slices on a baking sheet lined with parchment paper. Bake in the preheated oven for about 10-12 minutes or until the guanciale becomes crispy. Once done, remove from the oven and set aside.
3. Boil the Eggs: While the guanciale is baking, bring a pot of water to a boil. Gently add the eggs and boil for exactly 6 minutes. Then, remove the eggs and immediately transfer them to a bowl of ice water to halt the cooking process. Carefully peel the eggs and set them aside.
4. Assemble the Dish: Heat olive oil in a skillet over medium heat. Carefully place the soft-boiled eggs in the skillet and cook for 1-2 minutes, turning occasionally, until they develop a light golden crust.
5. Plate the Dish: Place each golden-crusted egg on individual serving plates. Crumble the crispy guanciale over the eggs, sprinkle generously

with grated Grana Padano cheese, and finish with a dash of freshly ground black pepper. Garnish with chopped chives if desired.

6. Serve: Serve immediately, allowing guests to cut into the soft eggs and relish the creamy yolk mingling with the crispy guanciale and the rich Grana Padano cheese.

Nutrition Information (per serving):
- Calories: 260
- Total Fat: 18g
- Saturated Fat: 7g
- Trans Fat: 0g
- Cholesterol: 225mg
- Sodium: 520mg
- Total Carbohydrate: 1g
- Dietary Fiber: 0g
- Sugars: 0g
- Protein: 20g

Please note that nutritional information may vary based on specific brands and quantities of ingredients used. Adjustments can be made to suit dietary preferences or restrictions. Enjoy this delightful dish inspired by the culinary wonders of Tom Douglas's Serious Pie restaurant!

30. Buffalo Mozzarella with Tomato Sauce & Basil

This delectable Buffalo Mozzarella with Tomato Sauce & Basil dish draws its inspiration from the tantalizing flavors found at Tom Douglas's Serious Pie restaurant. A harmonious blend of creamy buffalo mozzarella, vibrant tomato sauce, and fragrant basil creates a dish that celebrates simplicity and freshness, making it a standout choice for any occasion.

Serving: 4 servings
Preparation time: 10 minutes
Ready time: 15 minutes

Ingredients:
- 4 large slices of buffalo mozzarella
- 2 cups tomato sauce (homemade or store-bought)

- 1/4 cup fresh basil leaves, torn
- Salt and freshly ground black pepper, to taste
- Extra-virgin olive oil, for drizzling

Instructions:
1. Prepare the Ingredients: Ensure the buffalo mozzarella slices are at room temperature. If using homemade tomato sauce, warm it gently in a saucepan over low heat. Wash and tear the fresh basil leaves.
2. Preheat and Assemble: Preheat the oven to 375°F (190°C). Place the buffalo mozzarella slices on a baking dish or ovenproof plate, leaving space between each slice. Season the slices lightly with salt and pepper.
3. Warm the Mozzarella: Place the dish of buffalo mozzarella in the preheated oven and bake for 5-7 minutes or until the cheese begins to soften and slightly melt.
4. Warm the Tomato Sauce: Meanwhile, in a small saucepan, gently warm the tomato sauce over low to medium heat, stirring occasionally. Ensure it's hot but not boiling.
5. Assemble the Dish: Once the mozzarella slices are warmed and slightly melted, carefully remove the dish from the oven. Spoon the warm tomato sauce over each slice of mozzarella.
6. Garnish and Serve: Sprinkle torn basil leaves generously over the tomato sauce-topped mozzarella. Drizzle a touch of extra-virgin olive oil over the dish for added flavor.
7. Serve: Serve immediately while the cheese is warm and gooey, accompanied by crusty bread or a side salad, if desired.

Nutrition Information (per serving):
- Calories: 220
- Total Fat: 15g
- Saturated Fat: 8g
- Cholesterol: 45mg
- Sodium: 650mg
- Total Carbohydrates: 8g
- Dietary Fiber: 2g
- Sugars: 5g
- Protein: 15g

Note: Nutrition information is approximate and may vary based on specific ingredients used and serving sizes.

Enjoy the delightful blend of flavors in this Buffalo Mozzarella with Tomato Sauce & Basil, a dish that embodies the essence of simplicity and quality ingredients, reminiscent of the offerings at Tom Douglas's Serious Pie restaurant.

31. Penn Cove Clams with Garlic, Chili Flakes & Lemon

Penn Cove Clams with Garlic, Chili Flakes & Lemon is a delectable seafood dish that embodies the flavors of the Pacific Northwest. Inspired by the menu of Tom Douglas's renowned Serious Pie restaurant, this recipe offers a delightful combination of fresh clams, aromatic garlic, a hint of spice from chili flakes, and a zesty touch of lemon. It's a dish that celebrates the simplicity of quality ingredients and the vibrant flavors of the region.

Serving: 2-4 servings
Preparation time: 15 minutes
Ready time: 20 minutes

Ingredients:
- 2 pounds fresh Penn Cove clams, scrubbed clean
- 3 tablespoons olive oil
- 4 cloves garlic, thinly sliced
- ½ teaspoon red chili flakes (adjust to taste)
- Zest of 1 lemon
- Juice of 1 lemon
- ½ cup dry white wine
- 2 tablespoons chopped fresh parsley
- Salt and black pepper to taste
- Crusty bread, for serving

Instructions:
1. Preparation:
- Scrub the clams under cold running water to remove any dirt or sand. Discard any clams that are open and do not close when tapped lightly.
2. Sautéing the Aromatics:
- Heat the olive oil in a large, deep skillet or pot over medium heat.
- Add the sliced garlic and red chili flakes, sauté for about 1 minute until the garlic becomes fragrant. Be careful not to burn the garlic.

3. Cooking the Clams:
- Increase the heat to medium-high. Add the cleaned clams to the skillet.
- Pour in the white wine and lemon juice. Cover with a lid and cook for about 5-7 minutes or until the clams have opened. Discard any clams that do not open after cooking.
4. Finishing Touches:
- Once the clams have opened, remove the skillet from heat.
- Season the clams with salt and black pepper to taste. Add the lemon zest and chopped parsley. Gently toss to combine.
5. Serving:
- Transfer the cooked clams along with the flavorful broth into serving bowls.
- Serve immediately with crusty bread to soak up the delicious juices.

Nutrition Information:
(*Note: Nutritional values can vary based on specific ingredients used and serving sizes.*)
- Serving size: 1/4 of recipe
- Calories: Approximately 250-300
- Fat: Approximately 10-15g
- Protein: Approximately 20-25g
- Carbohydrates: Approximately 15-20g
- Fiber: Approximately 1-2g
Enjoy these Penn Cove Clams with Garlic, Chili Flakes & Lemon as a delightful appetizer or a main course that captures the essence of Pacific Northwest cuisine, delivering a burst of flavors in every bite.

32. Roasted Chanterelle Mushrooms with Truffle Cheese & Thyme

Indulge in the exquisite flavors of earthy chanterelle mushrooms enhanced by the richness of truffle cheese and the fragrant essence of thyme. This recipe draws inspiration from the tantalizing menu at Tom Douglas's Serious Pie restaurant, where culinary innovation meets savory delights. Roasting these mushrooms to perfection creates a dish that celebrates the simplicity and depth of flavors found in quality ingredients.

Serving: 4 servings
Preparation time: 15 minutes
Ready time: 30 minutes

Ingredients:
- 1 pound chanterelle mushrooms, cleaned and trimmed
- 2 tablespoons olive oil
- 2 cloves garlic, minced
- 1 tablespoon fresh thyme leaves
- Salt and pepper to taste
- 1/2 cup truffle cheese, grated
- Fresh thyme sprigs for garnish (optional)

Instructions:
1. Preheat the oven to 400°F (200°C). Line a baking sheet with parchment paper or lightly grease it.
2. Clean the chanterelle mushrooms thoroughly and trim off any tough or dirty parts. If they are large, you can cut them into bite-sized pieces for even roasting.
3. In a bowl, toss the cleaned chanterelle mushrooms with olive oil, minced garlic, fresh thyme leaves, salt, and pepper until evenly coated.
4. Spread the seasoned mushrooms in a single layer on the prepared baking sheet.
5. Roast the mushrooms in the preheated oven for about 20-25 minutes, or until they are golden brown and tender, stirring once halfway through the cooking time.
6. Once the mushrooms are roasted to perfection, remove them from the oven and sprinkle the grated truffle cheese over the hot mushrooms. Return the baking sheet to the oven for an additional 2-3 minutes, or until the cheese is melted and bubbly.
7. Carefully transfer the roasted chanterelle mushrooms with melted truffle cheese to a serving platter. Garnish with fresh thyme sprigs if desired and serve immediately.

Nutrition Information (approximate values per serving):
- Calories: 180
- Total Fat: 12g
- Saturated Fat: 4g
- Cholesterol: 15mg
- Sodium: 200mg

- Total Carbohydrate: 10g
- Dietary Fiber: 2g
- Sugars: 2g
- Protein: 8g

Note: Nutrition Information may vary based on specific ingredients used and portion sizes.

Enjoy this delectable dish of Roasted Chanterelle Mushrooms with Truffle Cheese & Thyme as a delightful appetizer or as a flavorful side dish to complement your main course.

33. Sweet Fennel Sausage with Roasted Red Pepper & Pecorino

Inspired by the delectable menu at Tom Douglas's Serious Pie restaurant, this recipe for Sweet Fennel Sausage with Roasted Red Pepper & Pecorino is a delightful fusion of flavors. Infused with the aromatic essence of fennel, complemented by the smoky sweetness of roasted red peppers and the richness of Pecorino cheese, this dish promises a savory experience that's both comforting and indulgent.

Serving: 4 servings
Preparation time: 15 minutes
Ready time: 45 minutes

Ingredients:
- 4 links sweet fennel sausage
- 2 red bell peppers
- 1 tablespoon olive oil
- Salt and pepper to taste
- ½ cup grated Pecorino cheese
- Fresh parsley leaves for garnish (optional)

Instructions:
1. Preheat the oven to 400°F (200°C).
2. Place the red bell peppers on a baking sheet and roast them in the oven for about 20-25 minutes, or until the skins are blistered and charred. Rotate the peppers occasionally for even roasting.

3. Remove the peppers from the oven and place them in a bowl. Cover the bowl with plastic wrap or a kitchen towel and let the peppers steam for about 10 minutes. This will make it easier to peel off the skins. Once cooled, peel off the skins, remove the seeds, and slice the peppers into thin strips.

4. While the peppers are cooling, heat a skillet over medium heat. Add the sweet fennel sausages to the skillet and cook, turning occasionally, until they are browned and cooked through, about 12-15 minutes.

5. In a separate pan, heat the olive oil over medium heat. Add the roasted red pepper strips to the pan, season with salt and pepper to taste, and sauté for 3-4 minutes until heated through.

6. Once the sausages are cooked, slice them diagonally into thick pieces.

7. To serve, place the sliced sausage on a serving platter or individual plates. Top the sausage with the sautéed roasted red pepper strips and sprinkle generously with grated Pecorino cheese.

8. Garnish with fresh parsley leaves if desired and serve hot.

Nutrition Information:
Note: Nutritional values may vary depending on specific ingredients and serving sizes.
- Calories per serving: Approximately 350 calories
- Total Fat: 25g
- Saturated Fat: 9g
- Cholesterol: 60mg
- Sodium: 900mg
- Total Carbohydrates: 5g
- Dietary Fiber: 1g
- Sugars: 3g
- Protein: 25g

Enjoy this flavorful combination of sweet fennel sausage, roasted red peppers, and Pecorino cheese for a satisfying meal that captures the essence of Serious Pie's inspired cuisine!

34. Soft Farm Egg, Prosciutto, Arugula & Pecorino with Olive Oil

This dish is an ode to the exquisite flavors served at Tom Douglas's Serious Pie restaurant. A harmonious combination of soft farm-fresh eggs, delicate prosciutto, peppery arugula, and flavorful pecorino cheese drizzled with the richness of olive oil. The simplicity of the ingredients allows each component to shine, creating a dish that tantalizes the taste buds and celebrates quality produce.

Serving: Serves 2
Preparation Time: 15 minutes
Ready Time: 15 minutes

Ingredients:
- 4 large farm eggs
- 4 slices of prosciutto
- 2 cups fresh arugula leaves
- 1/4 cup shaved Pecorino cheese
- 2 tablespoons extra-virgin olive oil
- Salt and freshly ground black pepper to taste

Instructions:
1. Prepare the Soft Farm Eggs:
- Bring a pot of water to a gentle boil. Carefully add the eggs and let them cook for 6 minutes. Remove the eggs and place them in an ice bath for 3-4 minutes to stop the cooking process. Carefully peel the eggs and set aside.
2. Assemble the Dish:
- Lay out the prosciutto slices on a serving plate.
- Arrange the fresh arugula leaves on top of the prosciutto slices.
3. Add the Soft Farm Eggs:
- Gently cut the soft-boiled eggs in half and place them on the bed of arugula.
4. Garnish and Drizzle:
- Sprinkle the shaved Pecorino cheese over the eggs and arugula.
- Drizzle the extra-virgin olive oil generously over the entire dish.
- Season with salt and freshly ground black pepper to taste.
5. Serve:
- Serve immediately, allowing the warmth of the eggs to slightly wilt the arugula. Enjoy the vibrant flavors and textures of this simple yet elegant dish.

Nutrition Information (per serving):
- Calories: 350

- Total Fat: 27g
- Saturated Fat: 8g
- Trans Fat: 0g
- Cholesterol: 385mg
- Sodium: 600mg
- Total Carbohydrates: 2g
- Dietary Fiber: 0.5g
- Sugars: 1g
- Protein: 25g

Nutritional values are approximate and may vary depending on ingredients used.

This dish encapsulates the essence of Tom Douglas's Serious Pie philosophy—simple, quality ingredients, and an appreciation for the interplay of flavors. Enjoy the luxurious simplicity of this farm-fresh egg dish, perfect for a delightful breakfast or a light, satisfying meal.

35. Anchovy & Soft Farm Egg with Tomato Sauce & Chili Flakes

Indulge your taste buds in a symphony of flavors with this delectable dish inspired by the renowned Serious Pie restaurant by Tom Douglas. The Anchovy & Soft Farm Egg with Tomato Sauce & Chili Flakes is a culinary masterpiece that harmonizes the rich umami of anchovies, the creaminess of a soft farm egg, and the bold kick of chili flakes. Elevate your dining experience with this sophisticated yet approachable recipe that captures the essence of Serious Pie's menu.

Serving: 2 servings
Preparation time: 15 minutes
Ready time: 25 minutes

Ingredients:
- 4 large farm eggs
- 1 can (2 oz) anchovy fillets in oil, drained
- 2 cups tomato sauce (homemade or store-bought)
- 1 teaspoon chili flakes (adjust to taste)
- 2 tablespoons olive oil
- Salt and pepper to taste

- Fresh basil leaves for garnish

Instructions:
1. Preheat the oven: Preheat your oven to 375°F (190°C).
2. Prepare the anchovies: Lay the anchovy fillets on a cutting board and finely chop them. Set aside.
3. Heat the tomato sauce: In a saucepan, heat the olive oil over medium heat. Add the chopped anchovies and sauté for 2-3 minutes until they begin to dissolve. Pour in the tomato sauce and add chili flakes. Stir well and let it simmer for 5-7 minutes, allowing the flavors to meld. Season with salt and pepper to taste.
4. Create wells for eggs: Using a spoon, make four wells in the tomato sauce mixture. Crack one egg into each well, ensuring the yolks remain intact.
5. Bake in the oven: Transfer the saucepan to the preheated oven and bake for 10-12 minutes or until the egg whites are set, but the yolks are still runny.
6. Garnish and serve: Carefully remove the saucepan from the oven. Garnish with fresh basil leaves and an extra sprinkle of chili flakes if desired. Serve immediately, allowing the runny yolk to mingle with the savory tomato sauce.

Nutrition Information (per serving):
- Calories: 320 kcal
- Protein: 15g
- Fat: 22g
- Carbohydrates: 18g
- Fiber: 4g
- Sugar: 12g
- Sodium: 880mg

Delight in the tantalizing blend of textures and tastes, as the creamy egg yolk, savory anchovies, and zesty tomato sauce come together in a gastronomic symphony that will transport you to the heart of Serious Pie's culinary experience.

36. Smoked Provolone, Tomato Sauce & Sweet Fennel Sausage with Chili Flakes

Indulge in the robust flavors inspired by Tom Douglas's renowned Serious Pie restaurant with this delectable recipe featuring Smoked Provolone, Tomato Sauce & Sweet Fennel Sausage with a hint of Chili Flakes. The melding of smoky provolone, zesty tomato sauce, and the savory essence of sweet fennel sausage creates a pizza experience that embodies the essence of Serious Pie's inventive menu.

Serving: 4 servings
Preparation Time: 15 minutes
Ready Time: 25 minutes

Ingredients:
- 1 pound pizza dough, at room temperature
- 1 cup tomato sauce
- 2 cups smoked provolone cheese, shredded
- 1 pound sweet fennel sausage, casing removed and crumbled
- 1 teaspoon chili flakes
- Fresh basil leaves for garnish (optional)
- Olive oil for drizzling

Instructions:
1. Preheat the Oven:
Preheat your oven to 500°F (260°C). If you have a pizza stone, place it in the oven during the preheating.
2. Prepare the Dough:
Roll out the pizza dough on a lightly floured surface to your desired thickness. If you prefer a thin crust, roll it out more, and for a thicker crust, keep it slightly thicker.
3. Assemble the Pizza:
Spread the tomato sauce evenly over the rolled-out pizza dough, leaving a small border around the edges. Sprinkle the shredded smoked provolone evenly over the sauce. Distribute the crumbled sweet fennel sausage over the cheese. Sprinkle chili flakes for a touch of heat.
4. Bake the Pizza:
If you have a pizza peel, transfer the assembled pizza onto the preheated pizza stone in the oven. If not, place the pizza on a parchment-lined baking sheet. Bake for approximately 12-15 minutes or until the crust is golden and the cheese is bubbly and slightly browned.
5. Finish and Garnish:

Once out of the oven, drizzle the pizza with a bit of olive oil for added richness. If desired, garnish with fresh basil leaves for a burst of freshness.

6. Slice and Serve:

Allow the pizza to cool for a few minutes before slicing. Serve hot and enjoy the delightful combination of smoky provolone, sweet fennel sausage, and the kick of chili flakes.

Nutrition Information:

(Note: Nutritional values are approximate and may vary based on specific ingredients and portion sizes.)

- Calories: 450 per serving
- Total Fat: 22g
- Saturated Fat: 10g
- Cholesterol: 60mg
- Sodium: 1100mg
- Total Carbohydrates: 40g
- Dietary Fiber: 2g
- Sugars: 3g
- Protein: 20g

Dive into the culinary world of Serious Pie with this Smoked Provolone, Tomato Sauce & Sweet Fennel Sausage pizza, a testament to the restaurant's commitment to bold and inventive flavors.

37. Guanciale, Castelvetrano Olives & Tomato Sauce with Chili Flakes

Indulge in the rustic flavors of Tom Douglas's Serious Pie restaurant with this tantalizing recipe for "Guanciale, Castelvetrano Olives & Tomato Sauce with Chili Flakes." This dish embodies the essence of Italian cuisine, featuring the richness of guanciale, the briny notes of Castelvetrano olives, and a zesty kick from chili flakes. Prepare to embark on a culinary journey that celebrates the artistry of flavors and textures inspired by the renowned Serious Pie menu.

Serving: 4 servings
Preparation Time: 15 minutes
Ready Time: 45 minutes

Ingredients:
- 1 pound spaghetti or your favorite pasta
- 1/4 cup extra-virgin olive oil
- 1/2 pound guanciale, thinly sliced
- 3 cloves garlic, minced
- 1 can (28 ounces) whole peeled tomatoes, crushed by hand
- 1 cup Castelvetrano olives, pitted and halved
- 1 teaspoon chili flakes (adjust to taste)
- Salt and black pepper to taste
- Grated Pecorino Romano cheese for garnish
- Fresh basil leaves for garnish

Instructions:
1. Bring a large pot of salted water to a boil. Cook the pasta according to package instructions until al dente. Reserve 1/2 cup of pasta cooking water before draining.
2. In a large skillet, heat the olive oil over medium heat. Add the guanciale slices and cook until they become crispy and golden brown, about 5 minutes.
3. Add minced garlic to the skillet and sauté for 1-2 minutes until fragrant.
4. Pour in the crushed tomatoes and their juices. Stir in Castelvetrano olives and chili flakes. Season with salt and black pepper to taste. Simmer the sauce for 20-25 minutes, allowing the flavors to meld and the sauce to thicken.
5. Toss the cooked pasta into the skillet, ensuring it's well-coated with the sauce. If needed, add some of the reserved pasta cooking water to achieve the desired consistency.
6. Serve the pasta in individual bowls, garnishing each with grated Pecorino Romano cheese and fresh basil leaves.

Nutrition Information:
(Per serving)
- Calories: 550
- Protein: 15g
- Fat: 22g
- Carbohydrates: 70g
- Fiber: 6g
- Sugar: 8g

- Sodium: 800mg

Elevate your dining experience with the bold and savory blend of guanciale, Castelvetrano olives, and a hint of chili flakes— a taste sensation that pays homage to the culinary excellence of Tom Douglas's Serious Pie.

38. Yukon Gold Potato, Rosemary & Caciocavallo with Olive Oil

Indulge your taste buds in the rustic charm of Tom Douglas's Serious Pie-inspired dish, featuring the sublime combination of Yukon Gold Potatoes, fragrant Rosemary, and the rich notes of Caciocavallo cheese, all elevated with a drizzle of extra-virgin Olive Oil. This culinary masterpiece captures the essence of Serious Pie's dedication to flavor and quality. Let the earthy potatoes, aromatic rosemary, and savory cheese take you on a journey through the heart of artisanal cuisine.

Serving: 4 servings
Preparation Time: 15 minutes
Ready Time: 40 minutes

Ingredients:
- 1.5 lbs Yukon Gold Potatoes, thinly sliced
- 2 tablespoons fresh Rosemary, finely chopped
- 1 cup Caciocavallo cheese, grated
- 1/4 cup extra-virgin Olive Oil
- Salt and black pepper to taste

Instructions:
1. Preheat the Oven:
Preheat your oven to 375°F (190°C).
2. Prepare the Potatoes:
Wash and scrub the Yukon Gold potatoes thoroughly. Slice them into thin rounds, ensuring uniform thickness for even cooking.
3. Layering:
In a baking dish, create a layer of overlapping potato slices. Sprinkle a portion of chopped rosemary and grated Caciocavallo cheese over the

potatoes. Drizzle a bit of olive oil, and season with salt and black pepper. Repeat this layering process until all the potatoes are used.

4. Final Touch:

Finish the top layer with an extra sprinkle of rosemary, cheese, and a generous drizzle of olive oil for a golden finish.

5. Bake:

Place the baking dish in the preheated oven. Bake for approximately 25-30 minutes or until the potatoes are tender and the cheese develops a delicious golden crust.

6. Serve:

Once out of the oven, let it cool for a few minutes before serving. This dish pairs wonderfully with a side salad or as a rustic accompaniment to your favorite protein.

Nutrition Information:

Note: Nutritional values are approximate and may vary based on specific ingredients used.

- Calories: 320 per serving
- Total Fat: 18g
- Saturated Fat: 7g
- Trans Fat: 0g
- Cholesterol: 30mg
- Sodium: 250mg
- Total Carbohydrates: 30g
- Dietary Fiber: 4g
- Sugars: 2g
- Protein: 12g

Delight in the warmth of Yukon Gold Potato, Rosemary & Caciocavallo with Olive Oil, a dish that embodies the soulful essence of Tom Douglas's Serious Pie restaurant. Enjoy the harmonious blend of textures and flavors in every savory bite.

39. Penn Cove Clams with House Pancetta & Lemon with Chili Flakes

Indulge your taste buds in the exquisite flavors of the Pacific Northwest with this enticing dish inspired by Tom Douglas's Serious Pie restaurant. Penn Cove Clams take center stage, their briny sweetness complemented by the rich, house-cured pancetta, bright lemon, and a hint of chili flakes. This recipe promises a symphony of flavors that celebrates the bounty of the sea and the culinary finesse of Serious Pie.

Serving: 4 servings
Preparation Time: 15 minutes
Ready Time: 30 minutes

Ingredients:
- 2 pounds Penn Cove Clams, scrubbed and cleaned
- 1/4 cup house-cured pancetta, diced
- 2 tablespoons olive oil
- 4 cloves garlic, minced
- 1/2 teaspoon chili flakes (adjust to taste)
- Zest of 1 lemon
- Juice of 1 lemon
- 1/4 cup fresh parsley, chopped
- Salt and black pepper to taste

Instructions:
1. Preheat and Prepare: Heat olive oil in a large, deep skillet over medium heat. Add the diced pancetta and cook until it becomes crispy and golden brown.
2. Sauté Aromatics: Add minced garlic to the skillet, sautéing until fragrant. The combination of garlic and pancetta will create a tantalizing aroma.
3. Clam Addition: Gently add the cleaned Penn Cove Clams to the skillet, stirring to coat them in the flavorful mixture.
4. Flavor Infusion: Sprinkle chili flakes over the clams for a subtle kick. Stir in the lemon zest, ensuring the zest is evenly distributed.
5. Steam and Simmer: Pour the lemon juice over the clams, cover the skillet, and allow the clams to steam and simmer for about 10-15 minutes or until they open. Discard any clams that remain closed.
6. Finish with Freshness: Season with salt and black pepper to taste. Sprinkle fresh parsley over the clams, adding a burst of color and herbaceousness.
7. Serve: Plate the clams in shallow bowls, spooning the broth over them. Serve with crusty bread to soak up the delicious juices.

Nutrition Information (per serving):

- Calories: 280
- Protein: 22g
- Carbohydrates: 10g
- Fat: 16g
- Saturated Fat: 4g
- Cholesterol: 65mg
- Fiber: 1g
- Sugar: 1g
- Sodium: 700mg

Celebrate the essence of Serious Pie with this Penn Cove Clams recipe, a delightful tribute to the culinary wonders of the Pacific Northwest.

40. Prosciutto, Pecorino & Arugula with Olive Oil & Chili Flakes

Indulge your taste buds with the vibrant and sophisticated flavors inspired by Tom Douglas's Serious Pie restaurant. This recipe for "Prosciutto, Pecorino & Arugula with Olive Oil & Chili Flakes" captures the essence of the restaurant's dedication to quality ingredients and inventive combinations. The delicate saltiness of prosciutto, the robust richness of Pecorino, and the peppery bite of arugula are beautifully enhanced by the warmth of olive oil and a hint of chili flakes. Elevate your culinary experience with this elegant and easy-to-make dish.

Serving: 2
Preparation time: 15 minutes
Ready time: 15 minutes

Ingredients:
- 8 slices of prosciutto
- 1 cup fresh arugula, washed and dried
- 1/2 cup Pecorino cheese, shaved
- 2 tablespoons extra-virgin olive oil
- 1/2 teaspoon chili flakes (adjust to taste)
- Freshly ground black pepper, to taste

Instructions:
1. Prepare the Ingredients:

- Lay out the prosciutto slices on a clean surface.
- Wash and dry the arugula thoroughly.
- Shave the Pecorino cheese into thin, delicate slices.
2. Assemble the Dish:
- Place 4 slices of prosciutto on each serving plate, arranging them in a visually appealing manner.
- Scatter a handful of fresh arugula over the prosciutto, ensuring an even distribution.
3. Add Pecorino and Season:
- Generously scatter shaved Pecorino over the prosciutto and arugula.
- Drizzle extra-virgin olive oil over the entire dish, ensuring each component gets a touch of the richness.
4. Finish with Chili Flakes:
- Sprinkle chili flakes over the dish, adding a subtle kick that complements the other flavors.
- Grind fresh black pepper on top to taste.
5. Serve:
- Serve immediately, allowing the prosciutto to showcase its delicate texture and the arugula to maintain its freshness.

Nutrition Information:
Note: Nutrition information is approximate and may vary based on specific ingredients used.
- Calories: 350 per serving
- Protein: 18g
- Fat: 28g
- Carbohydrates: 2g
- Fiber: 1g
- Sugar: 0g
- Sodium: 950mg
Indulge in the simplicity and sophistication of this Prosciutto, Pecorino & Arugula dish, a culinary masterpiece inspired by the renowned flavors of Tom Douglas's Serious Pie restaurant.

41. Buffalo Mozzarella with Tomato Sauce & Basil with Chili Flakes

Indulge in the rustic charm of Tom Douglas's Serious Pie restaurant with this delightful recipe for Buffalo Mozzarella with Tomato Sauce & Basil, enhanced with a hint of chili flakes. This dish captures the essence of the restaurant's commitment to quality ingredients and bold flavors. The creamy buffalo mozzarella paired with vibrant tomato sauce and fresh basil creates a symphony of tastes that will transport you straight to the heart of serious pizza perfection.

Serving: Serves 4
Preparation Time: 15 minutes
Ready Time: 25 minutes

Ingredients:
- 1 pound buffalo mozzarella, sliced
- 2 cups tomato sauce (homemade or store-bought)
- 1 cup fresh basil leaves, torn
- 1 teaspoon chili flakes (adjust to taste)
- Salt and pepper to taste
- 2 tablespoons olive oil

Instructions:
1. Preheat the Oven: Preheat your oven to 375°F (190°C).
2. Prepare the Mozzarella: Arrange the sliced buffalo mozzarella evenly on a baking dish or ovenproof platter.
3. Warm the Tomato Sauce: In a saucepan, heat the tomato sauce over medium heat. Season with salt and pepper to taste. Once heated through, pour the sauce evenly over the buffalo mozzarella slices.
4. Add Basil and Chili Flakes: Sprinkle torn fresh basil leaves over the mozzarella and tomato sauce. For a subtle kick, evenly distribute the chili flakes.
5. Bake to Perfection: Place the dish in the preheated oven and bake for 15-20 minutes, or until the cheese is melted and bubbly, and the edges are golden brown.
6. Drizzle with Olive Oil: Just before serving, drizzle the dish with olive oil for a touch of richness.
7. Serve and Enjoy: Remove from the oven, let it cool for a minute, and serve this savory delight with crusty bread or as a side to your favorite pizza.

Nutrition Information:

(Per Serving)
- Calories: 320
- Fat: 22g
- Saturated Fat: 12g
- Cholesterol: 60mg
- Sodium: 850mg
- Carbohydrates: 12g
- Fiber: 3g
- Sugars: 6g
- Protein: 20g

Indulge in the simplicity and bold flavors of this Buffalo Mozzarella with Tomato Sauce & Basil, a recipe that pays homage to the culinary excellence of Tom Douglas's Serious Pie restaurant.

42. Soft Farm Egg, Guanciale & Grana Padano with Olive Oil

Indulge in the sublime symphony of flavors with this exquisite dish inspired by the renowned Serious Pie restaurant. The Soft Farm Egg, Guanciale & Grana Padano with Olive Oil is a celebration of simple ingredients elevated to perfection. Tom Douglas's culinary influence shines through in this harmonious blend of farm-fresh eggs, savory guanciale, and the rich depth of Grana Padano, all brought together with a drizzle of premium olive oil.

Serving: Ideal for a sophisticated brunch or a luxurious appetizer, this dish serves 4.
Preparation Time: 15 minutes
Ready Time: 20 minutes

Ingredients:
- 4 farm-fresh eggs
- 150g guanciale, thinly sliced
- 100g Grana Padano, shaved
- 2 tablespoons extra-virgin olive oil
- Salt and black pepper to taste

Instructions:

1. Preheat the oven: Set your oven to 375°F (190°C).
2. Prepare the guanciale: In a skillet over medium heat, crisp up the guanciale slices until golden brown and irresistibly fragrant. Remove from heat and set aside.
3. Soft boil the eggs: Carefully place the eggs in a pot of boiling water and cook for exactly 6 minutes. Once done, transfer them to an ice bath to stop the cooking process. Gently peel the eggs and set aside.
4. Assemble the dish: On individual serving plates, arrange the soft-boiled eggs. Surround them with the crispy guanciale slices. Generously sprinkle shaved Grana Padano over the eggs.
5. Drizzle with olive oil: Finish the dish by drizzling each serving with extra-virgin olive oil. The oil adds a luscious, silky texture that ties all the elements together.
6. Season to perfection: Sprinkle with salt and freshly ground black pepper according to your taste.
7. Serve immediately: This dish is at its best when served fresh and warm. The creamy yolk, crispy guanciale, and nutty Grana Padano create a mouthwatering experience.

Nutrition Information:
Per serving (1/4 of the recipe):
- Calories: 320
- Protein: 15g
- Fat: 25g
- Carbohydrates: 2g
- Fiber: 0g
- Sugar: 0g
- Sodium: 500mg
Savor the sophistication of Serious Pie's culinary inspiration with each delectable bite of Soft Farm Egg, Guanciale & Grana Padano with Olive Oil. Elevate your dining experience with this masterpiece that embodies the essence of Tom Douglas's culinary artistry.

43. Sweet Fennel Sausage with Roasted Red Pepper & Pecorino with Chili Flakes

Indulge your taste buds in a symphony of flavors with this delectable dish inspired by the menu of Tom Douglas's renowned Serious Pie restaurant. The Sweet Fennel Sausage with Roasted Red Pepper & Pecorino with Chili Flakes combines savory sausage, smoky roasted red peppers, and the bold kick of chili flakes, all harmonizing with the richness of Pecorino cheese. This dish encapsulates the spirit of Serious Pie's inventive and scrumptious offerings.

Serving: 4 servings
Preparation Time: 15 minutes
Ready Time: 45 minutes

Ingredients:
- 1 pound sweet fennel sausage, casings removed
- 2 red bell peppers, roasted and sliced
- 1 cup Pecorino cheese, grated
- 1 teaspoon chili flakes (adjust to taste)
- 2 tablespoons olive oil
- Salt and black pepper to taste
- Fresh parsley, chopped (for garnish)

Instructions:
1. Preheat the Oven:
Preheat your oven to 400°F (200°C).
2. Roast the Red Peppers:
Place the red bell peppers on a baking sheet and roast in the preheated oven for 20-25 minutes or until the skin is charred. Remove from the oven, cover with a kitchen towel, and let them cool. Once cooled, peel off the skin, remove seeds, and slice the roasted peppers into thin strips.
3. Cook the Sausage:
In a large skillet over medium heat, add 1 tablespoon of olive oil. Crumble the sweet fennel sausage into the skillet and cook until browned and cooked through, breaking it apart with a spatula. Remove excess fat if necessary.
4. Combine Ingredients:
Add the roasted red pepper slices to the skillet with the sausage. Sprinkle chili flakes over the mixture and toss to combine. Cook for an additional 2-3 minutes to let the flavors meld.
5. Prepare Pecorino Topping:
In a separate bowl, toss the grated Pecorino cheese with the remaining olive oil.
6. Serve:

Divide the sausage and pepper mixture among serving plates. Top each portion with a generous sprinkle of Pecorino cheese and finish with a dash of black pepper. Garnish with chopped fresh parsley.

Nutrition Information:
Note: Nutrition information is approximate and may vary based on specific ingredients used.
- Calories per serving: XXX
- Protein: XXXg
- Carbohydrates: XXXg
- Fat: XXXg
- Fiber: XXXg
- Sugar: XXXg
- Sodium: XXXmg

Enjoy this Sweet Fennel Sausage with Roasted Red Pepper & Pecorino with Chili Flakes for a mouthwatering experience that captures the essence of Serious Pie's culinary brilliance!

44. Roasted Chanterelle Mushrooms with Truffle Cheese & Thyme with Chili Flakes

Elevate your taste buds with the exquisite flavors of Roasted Chanterelle Mushrooms with Truffle Cheese & Thyme, a dish inspired by the culinary artistry of Tom Douglas's Serious Pie restaurant. This delectable recipe combines earthy chanterelle mushrooms with the luxurious essence of truffle cheese, enhanced by the aromatic notes of thyme and a hint of chili flakes for a perfect balance of warmth and depth. It's a celebration of the finest ingredients, creating a dish that's both sophisticated and comforting.

Serving: 4 servings
Preparation time: 15 minutes
Ready time: 30 minutes

Ingredients:
- 1 pound chanterelle mushrooms, cleaned and trimmed
- 2 tablespoons olive oil
- 1 teaspoon fresh thyme leaves

- 1/2 teaspoon chili flakes (adjust to taste)
- Salt and pepper to taste
- 1 cup truffle cheese, shaved or grated
- Fresh thyme sprigs for garnish

Instructions:
1. Preheat the Oven:
Preheat your oven to 400°F (200°C).
2. Prepare the Mushrooms:
Clean the chanterelle mushrooms thoroughly and trim any tough ends. If the mushrooms are large, you can halve or quarter them for even roasting.
3. Season the Mushrooms:
In a large bowl, toss the chanterelle mushrooms with olive oil, fresh thyme leaves, chili flakes, salt, and pepper. Ensure that the mushrooms are well-coated with the seasonings.
4. Roast the Mushrooms:
Spread the seasoned mushrooms in a single layer on a baking sheet. Roast in the preheated oven for 20-25 minutes or until the mushrooms are golden brown and tender, tossing them halfway through the cooking time for even roasting.
5. Add Truffle Cheese:
Once the mushrooms are roasted, sprinkle the shaved or grated truffle cheese over them while they are still hot. The residual heat will melt the cheese slightly, creating a luxurious coating.
6. Garnish and Serve:
Transfer the roasted chanterelle mushrooms with truffle cheese to a serving dish. Garnish with fresh thyme sprigs for a pop of color and added aroma. Serve immediately and savor the rich flavors.

Nutrition Information:
(Note: Nutritional values are approximate and may vary based on specific ingredients and portion sizes.)
- Calories: 220 per serving
- Fat: 15g
- Saturated Fat: 6g
- Cholesterol: 25mg
- Sodium: 180mg
- Carbohydrates: 12g
- Fiber: 3g

- Sugar: 2g
- Protein: 10g

Indulge in the irresistible allure of Roasted Chanterelle Mushrooms with Truffle Cheese & Thyme, a dish that embodies the culinary finesse of Tom Douglas's Serious Pie restaurant. Each bite is a symphony of earthy, savory, and aromatic notes, making it a standout addition to your gastronomic repertoire.

45. Hazelnut Brown Butter Cake with Caramel Sauce

Indulge your taste buds in the decadent world of Tom Douglas's Serious Pie with our Hazelnut Brown Butter Cake with Caramel Sauce. This sumptuous dessert captures the essence of Serious Pie's commitment to bold flavors and impeccable craftsmanship. The rich nuttiness of hazelnuts, the depth of brown butter, and the silky embrace of caramel come together in a harmonious symphony of taste. Elevate your culinary experience with this delightful treat that pays homage to the renowned flavors of Serious Pie.

Serving: Serves 8
Preparation Time: 20 minutes
Ready Time: 1 hour 30 minutes

Ingredients:
For the Hazelnut Brown Butter Cake:
- 1 cup unsalted butter
- 1 cup all-purpose flour
- 1 cup hazelnut meal
- 1 teaspoon baking powder
- 1/2 teaspoon salt
- 1 cup granulated sugar
- 4 large eggs
- 1 teaspoon vanilla extract
- 1/2 cup whole milk
For the Caramel Sauce:
- 1 cup granulated sugar
- 1/4 cup water

- 1/2 cup heavy cream
- 1/4 cup unsalted butter
- 1/2 teaspoon sea salt

Instructions:
Hazelnut Brown Butter Cake:
1. Preheat the oven to 350°F (175°C). Grease and flour a 9-inch round cake pan.
2. In a saucepan over medium heat, melt the butter. Continue to cook, stirring frequently until the butter turns golden brown and has a nutty aroma. Remove from heat and let it cool.
3. In a bowl, whisk together the flour, hazelnut meal, baking powder, and salt.
4. In a separate bowl, beat together the brown butter and sugar until light and fluffy.
5. Add the eggs one at a time, beating well after each addition. Stir in the vanilla extract.
6. Gradually add the dry ingredients to the wet ingredients, alternating with the milk. Begin and end with the dry ingredients, mixing until just combined.
7. Pour the batter into the prepared pan and smooth the top. Bake for 25-30 minutes or until a toothpick inserted into the center comes out clean.
8. Allow the cake to cool in the pan for 10 minutes before transferring it to a wire rack to cool completely.
Caramel Sauce:
1. In a medium saucepan, combine the sugar and water over medium heat. Swirl the pan occasionally until the sugar dissolves.
2. Once the sugar has dissolved, increase the heat to high and boil without stirring until the mixture turns a deep amber color.
3. Remove the pan from heat and carefully add the heavy cream, stirring continuously. Be cautious, as the mixture will bubble.
4. Stir in the butter and sea salt until smooth.
5. Allow the caramel sauce to cool slightly before drizzling it over the cooled hazelnut brown butter cake.

Nutrition Information:
Per Serving:
- Calories: 480
- Fat: 32g

- Saturated Fat: 17g
- Cholesterol: 150mg
- Sodium: 280mg
- Carbohydrates: 45g
- Fiber: 2g
- Sugar: 32g
- Protein: 7g
Note: Nutrition information is approximate and may vary based on specific ingredients and serving sizes.

46. Penn Cove Clams with Garlic, Chili Flakes & Lemon with Olive Oil

Indulge in the tantalizing flavors inspired by the renowned Serious Pie restaurant by Tom Douglas with our exquisite recipe for Penn Cove Clams with Garlic, Chili Flakes & Lemon in Olive Oil. This dish embodies the essence of the Pacific Northwest, combining the freshness of Penn Cove clams with the zesty kick of garlic, the subtle heat of chili flakes, and the bright acidity of lemon, all brought together with the richness of olive oil. Elevate your culinary experience with this simple yet sophisticated seafood delight that pays homage to the culinary expertise of Serious Pie.

Serving: 4 servings
Preparation Time: 15 minutes
Ready Time: 25 minutes

Ingredients:
- 2 pounds Penn Cove clams, scrubbed and cleaned
- 3 tablespoons olive oil
- 4 cloves garlic, minced
- 1 teaspoon chili flakes (adjust to taste)
- Zest of 1 lemon
- Juice of 1 lemon
- Salt and pepper to taste
- Fresh parsley, chopped, for garnish

Instructions:

1. Prepare the Clams:
- Scrub the clams under cold running water to remove any grit or debris.
- Discard any clams with broken shells or that do not close when tapped.
2. Sauté the Aromatics:
- In a large skillet or sauté pan, heat olive oil over medium heat.
- Add minced garlic and chili flakes, sautéing until the garlic is fragrant but not browned.
3. Cook the Clams:
- Increase the heat to medium-high and add the cleaned clams to the pan.
- Stir to coat the clams in the garlic and chili-infused oil.
- Pour in the lemon juice and add lemon zest, ensuring an even distribution of flavors.
- Cover the pan and cook for 8-10 minutes or until the clams have opened. Discard any unopened clams.
4. Season and Garnish:
- Season the dish with salt and pepper to taste.
- Garnish with fresh chopped parsley for a burst of color and freshness.
5. Serve:
- Spoon the clams and sauce into serving bowls, making sure to distribute the garlic, chili flakes, and lemon zest evenly.
- Serve immediately, accompanied by crusty bread or over a bed of linguine for a more substantial meal.

Nutrition Information:
(Per Serving)
- Calories: 220
- Protein: 22g
- Fat: 11g
- Carbohydrates: 8g
- Fiber: 1g
- Sugar: 1g
- Sodium: 650mg
Savor the essence of the Pacific Northwest with this delightful clam dish that captures the essence of Tom Douglas's Serious Pie restaurant. Enjoy the harmonious blend of garlic, chili, lemon, and olive oil that elevates these Penn Cove clams to a level of culinary excellence.

47. Finocchiona Salami, Castelvetrano Olives & Tomato with Chili Flakes

Indulge in the vibrant flavors inspired by Tom Douglas's Serious Pie restaurant with this enticing dish of Finocchiona Salami, Castelvetrano Olives, and Tomatoes with a hint of Chili Flakes. This delightful combination showcases the essence of quality ingredients and culinary craftsmanship that defines Serious Pie's menu. Whether you're hosting a gathering or savoring a moment of culinary exploration, this recipe promises a burst of Italian-inspired goodness that captivates the senses.

Serving: Ideal for sharing as an appetizer or as a flavorful addition to a charcuterie board, this dish serves 4.
Preparation Time: 15 minutes
Ready Time: 15 minutes

Ingredients:
- 200g Finocchiona Salami, thinly sliced
- 1 cup Castelvetrano Olives, pitted and halved
- 1 cup Cherry Tomatoes, halved
- 1 teaspoon Chili Flakes (adjust to taste)
- 2 tablespoons Extra Virgin Olive Oil
- Fresh Basil leaves for garnish
- Salt and pepper to taste

Instructions:
1. Prepare the Ingredients:
- Slice the Finocchiona Salami thinly.
- Pit and halve the Castelvetrano Olives.
- Halve the Cherry Tomatoes.
2. Assemble the Dish:
- In a large serving bowl or platter, arrange the sliced Finocchiona Salami, halved Castelvetrano Olives, and Cherry Tomatoes.
3. Add a Kick of Spice:
- Sprinkle Chili Flakes evenly over the ingredients. Adjust the quantity according to your spice preference.
4. Drizzle with Olive Oil:
- Drizzle Extra Virgin Olive Oil over the assembled ingredients for a luscious finish.

5. Season to Perfection:
- Season with salt and pepper to taste.
6. Garnish:
- Garnish the dish with fresh Basil leaves for a burst of aromatic freshness.
7. Serve and Enjoy:
- Toss the ingredients gently to combine flavors and serve immediately. This dish pairs wonderfully with crusty bread or as part of a charcuterie spread.

Nutrition Information:
(Per Serving)
- Calories: 280
- Protein: 15g
- Fat: 22g
- Carbohydrates: 8g
- Fiber: 2g
- Sugar: 3g
- Sodium: 1100mg
Note: Nutrition information is approximate and may vary based on specific ingredients used.
Elevate your culinary experience with this Finocchiona Salami, Castelvetrano Olives, and Tomato with Chili Flakes dish—an homage to the exquisite flavors found at Tom Douglas's Serious Pie restaurant.

48. Buffalo Mozzarella, San Marzano Tomato & Basil with Chili Flakes

Indulge your taste buds in a symphony of flavors with this delectable dish inspired by the renowned Serious Pie restaurant, helmed by the culinary genius Tom Douglas. Our Buffalo Mozzarella, San Marzano Tomato & Basil with Chili Flakes recipe captures the essence of Serious Pie's commitment to fresh, high-quality ingredients and bold combinations. This simple yet sophisticated dish is a celebration of the vibrant flavors found in the heart of Italian cuisine.

Serving: Ideal for 2-4 people.
Preparation Time: 15 minutes

Ready Time: 15 minutes

Ingredients:
- 1 pound fresh Buffalo Mozzarella, sliced
- 1 pound ripe San Marzano tomatoes, sliced
- Fresh basil leaves, for garnish
- Red chili flakes, to taste
- Extra-virgin olive oil, for drizzling
- Sea salt and black pepper, to taste

Instructions:
1. Preheat Oven: Set your oven to broil.
2. Slice and Arrange: Slice the Buffalo Mozzarella and San Marzano tomatoes into even, medium-thin slices.
3. Assemble on Oven-safe Dish: Arrange the slices alternately in a circular pattern on an oven-safe dish, creating a visually appealing presentation.
4. Sprinkle with Chili Flakes: Sprinkle the dish with red chili flakes, adding a hint of heat to complement the richness of the mozzarella and sweetness of the tomatoes.
5. Broil Until Bubbly: Place the dish in the preheated oven and broil for 5-7 minutes or until the cheese is bubbly and slightly golden.
6. Garnish and Season: Remove from the oven and garnish with fresh basil leaves. Drizzle with extra-virgin olive oil and season with sea salt and black pepper to taste.
7. Serve: Serve immediately, allowing the melted mozzarella to create a sumptuous, gooey texture that blends perfectly with the juicy San Marzano tomatoes.

Nutrition Information:
Note: Nutritional values are approximate and may vary based on specific ingredients used.
- Calories: 250 per serving
- Protein: 18g
- Carbohydrates: 5g
- Fat: 18g
- Fiber: 2g
- Sugar: 3g

Elevate your culinary experience with this Buffalo Mozzarella, San Marzano Tomato & Basil with Chili Flakes dish—a homage to the exquisite offerings of Serious Pie. A true embodiment of simplicity and sophistication on a plate.

49. Wild Mushrooms with Truffle Cheese with Chili Flakes

Indulge your taste buds in a symphony of flavors with this exquisite dish inspired by the innovative menu of Tom Douglas's Serious Pie restaurant. Our "Wild Mushrooms with Truffle Cheese and Chili Flakes" is a culinary adventure that combines the earthy richness of wild mushrooms, the luxurious essence of truffle cheese, and a subtle kick of heat from chili flakes. This recipe promises to elevate your dining experience to a whole new level, capturing the essence of Serious Pie's commitment to exceptional ingredients and bold flavors.

Serving: 4 servings
Preparation Time: 15 minutes
Ready Time: 30 minutes

Ingredients:
- 1 pound mixed wild mushrooms (such as chanterelles, shiitake, and oyster mushrooms), cleaned and sliced
- 2 tablespoons olive oil
- 3 cloves garlic, minced
- Salt and black pepper to taste
- 1/2 cup truffle cheese, shaved or grated
- 1 teaspoon chili flakes (adjust to taste)
- 2 tablespoons fresh parsley, chopped (for garnish)

Instructions:
1. Preheat the pan: Heat olive oil in a large skillet over medium heat.
2. Sauté the mushrooms: Add the sliced wild mushrooms to the pan and sauté until they are golden brown and any liquid released has evaporated, about 8-10 minutes.
3. Season with garlic, salt, and pepper: Stir in the minced garlic and season the mushrooms with salt and black pepper to taste. Continue to sauté for an additional 2-3 minutes until the garlic is fragrant.

4. Add truffle cheese and chili flakes: Sprinkle the shaved or grated truffle cheese over the mushrooms, allowing it to melt and create a luscious coating. Add chili flakes for a hint of spice.

5. Combine and garnish: Gently toss the mushrooms until the cheese is evenly distributed, and the mushrooms are coated in the truffle goodness. Remove from heat.

6. Serve: Transfer the wild mushrooms to a serving dish, garnish with fresh parsley, and serve immediately.

Nutrition Information:
(Per Serving)
- Calories: 180
- Total Fat: 12g
- Saturated Fat: 4g
- Cholesterol: 15mg
- Sodium: 250mg
- Total Carbohydrates: 15g
- Dietary Fiber: 3g
- Sugars: 2g
- Protein: 8g

Delight your senses with this sophisticated dish that marries the untamed flavors of wild mushrooms with the decadence of truffle cheese and a touch of heat. A celebration of Tom Douglas's culinary expertise, this recipe promises a journey of flavors that will leave you craving more.

50. Soft Farm Egg, Prosciutto, Arugula & Pecorino with Olive Oil & Chili Flakes

Indulge in the exquisite flavors of Tom Douglas's Serious Pie restaurant with this delectable dish featuring soft farm eggs, savory prosciutto, peppery arugula, and flavorful Pecorino cheese drizzled with olive oil and a hint of chili flakes. This dish embodies the restaurant's commitment to using fresh, high-quality ingredients and simple yet bold flavors.

Serving: 2 servings
Preparation time: 10 minutes
Ready time: 15 minutes

Ingredients:
- 4 large farm eggs
- 4 slices of prosciutto
- 2 cups arugula, washed and dried
- 1/4 cup shaved Pecorino cheese
- 2 tablespoons extra-virgin olive oil
- Pinch of chili flakes
- Salt and black pepper to taste

Instructions:
1. Prepare the Ingredients:
- Bring a pot of water to a gentle simmer. Carefully add the eggs and cook for 6-7 minutes for a soft, runny yolk. Remove the eggs with a slotted spoon and place them in a bowl of ice water for a minute before peeling. Set aside.
- Heat a skillet over medium heat. Place the prosciutto slices in the skillet and cook for 1-2 minutes on each side until lightly crispy. Remove from the skillet and set aside.
2. Assemble the Dish:
- Arrange a handful of arugula on each serving plate.
3. Prepare the Soft Farm Eggs:
- Carefully cut the top off each soft-boiled egg and gently place them on the arugula bed.
4. Add Prosciutto and Pecorino:
- Crumble or tear the crispy prosciutto over the eggs.
- Sprinkle the shaved Pecorino cheese on top.
5. Drizzle with Olive Oil and Chili Flakes:
- Drizzle extra-virgin olive oil over the dish.
- Sprinkle a pinch of chili flakes for a touch of heat.
6. Season and Serve:
- Season lightly with salt and freshly ground black pepper to taste.

Nutrition Information (per serving):
- Calories: Approximately 300
- Protein: 18g
- Fat: 23g
- Carbohydrates: 2g
- Fiber: 1g
- Sodium: 650mg
- Sugar: 1g

Note: Nutritional values are approximate and may vary depending on specific ingredients used.

51. Anchovy & Soft Farm Egg with Tomato Sauce & Chili Flakes with Olive Oil

This recipe pays homage to the delectable offerings of Tom Douglas's Serious Pie restaurant, presenting a flavorful combination of savory anchovies, soft farm eggs, tangy tomato sauce, and a hint of heat from chili flakes with a drizzle of olive oil. The dish promises a delightful blend of rich flavors and textures that are sure to captivate your taste buds.

Serving: This recipe serves 2.
Preparation Time: 10 minutes
Ready Time: 20 minutes

Ingredients:
- 4 large farm eggs
- 8-10 anchovy fillets, preferably in oil, drained
- 1 cup tomato sauce
- 1 teaspoon chili flakes (adjust to taste)
- 2 tablespoons olive oil
- Salt and pepper to taste

Instructions:
1. Preparation:
- Preheat the oven to 375°F (190°C).
- In two individual-sized oven-safe dishes or small cast-iron skillets, evenly spread half a cup of tomato sauce in each dish.
2. Adding Anchovies and Eggs:
- Place 4-5 anchovy fillets on top of the tomato sauce in each dish.
- Gently crack 2 eggs into each dish, ensuring they rest on top of the anchovies and sauce without breaking the yolks.
3. Seasoning:
- Sprinkle chili flakes over the eggs, distributing them evenly.
- Season with a pinch of salt and a dash of pepper to your taste preference.

4. Bake:
- Place the dishes in the preheated oven and bake for approximately 12-15 minutes or until the egg whites are set, but the yolks remain slightly runny.
5. Finish:
- Once done, remove the dishes from the oven.
- Drizzle 1 tablespoon of olive oil over each dish.
6. Serve:
- Serve immediately, allowing the richness of the soft eggs, savory anchovies, and spicy tomato sauce to delight your palate.

Nutrition Information:
- *Note: Nutritional values are approximate and may vary based on specific ingredients used.*
- Calories per serving: Approximately 300-350 kcal
- Protein: 18-20g
- Fat: 20-25g
- Carbohydrates: 8-10g
- Fiber: 2-3g
Enjoy this savory and satisfying dish inspired by the renowned flavors of Tom Douglas's Serious Pie restaurant!

52. Smoked Provolone, Tomato Sauce & Sweet Fennel Sausage with Chili Flakes & Olive Oil

This recipe for "Smoked Provolone, Tomato Sauce & Sweet Fennel Sausage with Chili Flakes & Olive Oil" is a flavorful homage to the delightful offerings of Tom Douglas's Serious Pie restaurant. It brings together the smoky richness of provolone cheese, the tangy sweetness of tomato sauce, the savory notes of sweet fennel sausage, and the subtle kick of chili flakes, all drizzled with a finishing touch of olive oil. This dish embodies the restaurant's dedication to creating innovative and delicious pizza combinations that captivate the taste buds.

Serving: - Serves: 4
- Serving Size: 1 pizza
Preparation Time: - Prep Time: 20 minutes
Ready Time: - Ready In: 40 minutes

Ingredients:
- 1 pound pizza dough, at room temperature
- 1 cup tomato sauce
- 8 ounces smoked provolone cheese, shredded
- 8 ounces sweet fennel sausage, cooked and crumbled
- 1 teaspoon chili flakes (adjust to taste)
- 2 tablespoons olive oil

Instructions:
1. Preheat your oven to 500°F (260°C) and place a pizza stone or baking sheet inside to heat.
2. On a lightly floured surface, roll out the pizza dough into a circle or rectangle, about 1/4 inch thick.
3. Spread the tomato sauce evenly over the dough, leaving a border around the edges for the crust.
4. Sprinkle the shredded smoked provolone cheese over the tomato sauce.
5. Distribute the cooked and crumbled sweet fennel sausage evenly across the pizza.
6. Sprinkle chili flakes over the pizza for a touch of heat (adjust to your preferred spice level).
7. Carefully transfer the assembled pizza onto the preheated pizza stone or baking sheet.
8. Bake in the preheated oven for 12-15 minutes or until the crust is golden brown and the cheese is bubbly and slightly browned.
9. Once out of the oven, drizzle the pizza with olive oil for added richness and flavor.
10. Allow the pizza to cool for a minute or two before slicing.
11. Serve hot and enjoy this delicious creation inspired by Tom Douglas's Serious Pie!

Nutrition Information:
- Serving Size: 1 pizza
- Calories: Nutrition information may vary based on specific ingredients and portion sizes used.
- Fat: Nutrition information may vary based on specific ingredients and portion sizes used.
- Carbohydrates: Nutrition information may vary based on specific ingredients and portion sizes used.

- Protein: Nutrition information may vary based on specific ingredients and portion sizes used.
Note: Nutritional values are approximate and can vary based on ingredients and portion sizes used.
This delightful pizza encapsulates the essence of Serious Pie's innovative approach to flavor combinations and will undoubtedly become a favorite for pizza enthusiasts seeking a delicious, gourmet experience.

53. Guanciale, Castelvetrano Olives & Tomato Sauce with Chili Flakes & Olive Oil

Indulge your taste buds in a symphony of flavors with this exquisite recipe inspired by the menu of Tom Douglas's Serious Pie restaurant. Our Guanciale, Castelvetrano Olives & Tomato Sauce with Chili Flakes & Olive Oil is a celebration of premium ingredients, expertly combined to create a dish that's both comforting and sophisticated. The richness of guanciale, the buttery goodness of Castelvetrano olives, and the zing of chili flakes dance together in perfect harmony, elevated by the finest olive oil. Get ready to embark on a culinary journey that mirrors the culinary excellence of Serious Pie.

Serving: 4 servings
Preparation Time: 15 minutes
Ready Time: 45 minutes

Ingredients:
- 1/2 cup extra-virgin olive oil
- 150g guanciale, thinly sliced
- 2 cloves garlic, minced
- 1 teaspoon chili flakes (adjust to taste)
- 1 can (28 oz) crushed tomatoes
- 1 cup Castelvetrano olives, pitted and halved
- Salt and black pepper to taste
- 400g pasta of your choice (spaghetti or bucatini recommended)
- Fresh basil leaves for garnish (optional)
- Grated Pecorino Romano cheese for serving

Instructions:

1. In a large skillet, heat the olive oil over medium heat. Add the guanciale slices and cook until they become crispy and golden brown. Remove the guanciale from the pan and set it aside on a plate lined with paper towels to drain excess oil.
2. In the same skillet, add minced garlic and chili flakes. Sauté for about 1 minute until the garlic becomes fragrant.
3. Pour in the crushed tomatoes, stirring to combine with the garlic and chili flakes. Season with salt and black pepper to taste. Allow the sauce to simmer over medium-low heat for 20-30 minutes, allowing the flavors to meld.
4. While the sauce is simmering, cook the pasta according to package instructions until al dente. Drain and set aside.
5. Add the Castelvetrano olives and the cooked guanciale to the tomato sauce. Stir to combine and let it simmer for an additional 5 minutes.
6. Toss the cooked pasta in the sauce until well-coated. If needed, add a splash of pasta water to achieve your desired consistency.
7. Serve the pasta in bowls, garnished with fresh basil leaves if desired. Top with grated Pecorino Romano cheese.

Nutrition Information:
(Per Serving)
- Calories: 600
- Total Fat: 28g
- Saturated Fat: 6g
- Cholesterol: 20mg
- Sodium: 800mg
- Total Carbohydrates: 70g
- Dietary Fiber: 5g
- Sugars: 8g
- Protein: 18g

Immerse yourself in the sumptuousness of Serious Pie's culinary legacy with this Guanciale, Castelvetrano Olives & Tomato Sauce. A masterpiece on your plate, crafted with love and inspired by the artistry of Tom Douglas's kitchen.

54. Yukon Gold Potato, Rosemary & Caciocavallo with Olive Oil & Chili Flakes

Indulge in the rustic charm of Tom Douglas's Serious Pie with this delectable Yukon Gold Potato, Rosemary & Caciocavallo dish. Inspired by the renowned restaurant's commitment to bold flavors and quality ingredients, this recipe encapsulates the essence of Serious Pie's culinary excellence. The marriage of creamy Yukon Gold potatoes, fragrant rosemary, rich Caciocavallo cheese, and the kick of chili flakes, all drizzled with extra virgin olive oil, results in a dish that is both comforting and sophisticated.

Serving: 4 servings
Preparation Time: 15 minutes
Ready Time: 45 minutes

Ingredients:
- 4 large Yukon Gold potatoes, thinly sliced
- 1 cup Caciocavallo cheese, shredded
- 2 tablespoons fresh rosemary, finely chopped
- 1 teaspoon chili flakes (adjust to taste)
- 1/4 cup extra virgin olive oil
- Salt and black pepper to taste

Instructions:
1. Preheat the Oven:
Preheat your oven to 375°F (190°C).
2. Prepare Potatoes:
Wash and thinly slice the Yukon Gold potatoes. You can use a mandoline for uniform slices.
3. Layering:
In a baking dish, create layers of sliced potatoes, sprinkling each layer with Caciocavallo cheese, rosemary, chili flakes, salt, and black pepper.
4. Repeat:
Continue layering until all the potatoes are used, ensuring the top layer is covered with a generous amount of cheese and herbs.
5. Drizzle with Olive Oil:
Drizzle the assembled layers with extra virgin olive oil, ensuring an even distribution over the top.
6. Bake:
Place the baking dish in the preheated oven and bake for approximately 30-35 minutes or until the potatoes are tender and the top is golden brown.

7. Serve:

Once done, remove from the oven and let it rest for a few minutes. Serve the dish hot, allowing the flavors to meld together.

Nutrition Information:

Note: Nutrition information is approximate and may vary based on specific ingredients used and portion sizes.
- *Calories:* 350 per serving
- *Protein:* 10g
- *Fat:* 18g
- *Carbohydrates:* 40g
- *Fiber:* 5g
- *Sodium:* 400mg

Elevate your dining experience with the inviting aroma and exquisite taste of Yukon Gold Potato, Rosemary & Caciocavallo with Olive Oil & Chili Flakes – a culinary gem inspired by the menu of Tom Douglas's Serious Pie.

55. Penn Cove Clams with House Pancetta & Lemon with Chili Flakes & Olive Oil

Delight your taste buds with the exquisite flavors of Penn Cove Clams paired with house pancetta, brightened with the zing of lemon, and kissed with a hint of chili flakes and olive oil. This recipe draws inspiration from the culinary brilliance of Tom Douglas's Serious Pie restaurant, capturing the essence of their innovative and mouthwatering creations. The marriage of fresh clams and savory pancetta, elevated by the citrusy notes of lemon and the subtle heat of chili flakes, promises a dining experience that's both comforting and sophisticated.

Serving: 4
Preparation time: 15 minutes
Ready time: 30 minutes

Ingredients:
- 2 pounds Penn Cove clams, cleaned and scrubbed
- 1/4 cup house pancetta, diced
- 2 tablespoons olive oil

- 2 cloves garlic, minced
- Zest of 1 lemon
- Juice of 1 lemon
- 1/2 teaspoon chili flakes (adjust to taste)
- Salt and black pepper, to taste
- Fresh parsley, chopped, for garnish

Instructions:
1. Prepare the Clams:
- Rinse the Penn Cove clams thoroughly under cold water, scrubbing away any grit or debris. Discard any open or damaged clams.
- Soak the clams in cold water for 10 minutes to allow them to expel any sand.
2. Cook the Pancetta:
- In a large, deep skillet, cook the diced pancetta over medium heat until it turns golden brown and crispy. Remove excess fat, leaving about a tablespoon in the skillet.
3. Sauté Aromatics:
- Add minced garlic to the skillet with pancetta fat and sauté for 1-2 minutes until fragrant.
4. Cook the Clams:
- Add the cleaned clams to the skillet, stirring to coat them in the pancetta and garlic mixture.
- Pour in the olive oil, lemon zest, lemon juice, and chili flakes. Season with salt and black pepper to taste.
- Cover the skillet and cook for 8-10 minutes or until the clams have opened. Discard any clams that remain closed.
5. Garnish and Serve:
- Sprinkle chopped fresh parsley over the clams for a burst of color and added freshness.
- Serve the Penn Cove Clams with crusty bread to soak up the flavorful broth.

Nutrition Information:
Note: Nutrition information is approximate and may vary based on specific ingredients and serving sizes.
- Calories: 280 per serving
- Protein: 18g
- Fat: 15g
- Carbohydrates: 18g

- Fiber: 1g
- Sugar: 1g
- Sodium: 800mg

This Penn Cove Clams with House Pancetta & Lemon recipe offers a symphony of flavors that dance on your palate, making it a standout dish inspired by the culinary mastery of Tom Douglas's Serious Pie restaurant. Enjoy the richness of the sea, the smokiness of pancetta, and the brightness of citrus in every delectable bite.

56. Prosciutto, Pecorino & Arugula with Olive Oil & Chili Flakes

Indulge your taste buds with the vibrant and sophisticated flavors inspired by Tom Douglas's Serious Pie restaurant. This recipe for "Prosciutto, Pecorino & Arugula with Olive Oil & Chili Flakes" captures the essence of the restaurant's dedication to quality ingredients and inventive combinations. The delicate saltiness of prosciutto, the robust richness of Pecorino, and the peppery bite of arugula are beautifully enhanced by the warmth of olive oil and a hint of chili flakes. Elevate your culinary experience with this elegant and easy-to-make dish.

Serving: 2
Preparation time: 15 minutes
Ready time: 15 minutes

Ingredients:
- 8 slices of prosciutto
- 1 cup fresh arugula, washed and dried
- 1/2 cup Pecorino cheese, shaved
- 2 tablespoons extra-virgin olive oil
- 1/2 teaspoon chili flakes (adjust to taste)
- Freshly ground black pepper, to taste

Instructions:
1. Prepare the Ingredients:
- Lay out the prosciutto slices on a clean surface.
- Wash and dry the arugula thoroughly.
- Shave the Pecorino cheese into thin, delicate slices.

2. Assemble the Dish:
- Place 4 slices of prosciutto on each serving plate, arranging them in a visually appealing manner.
- Scatter a handful of fresh arugula over the prosciutto, ensuring an even distribution.
3. Add Pecorino and Season:
- Generously scatter shaved Pecorino over the prosciutto and arugula.
- Drizzle extra-virgin olive oil over the entire dish, ensuring each component gets a touch of the richness.
4. Finish with Chili Flakes:
- Sprinkle chili flakes over the dish, adding a subtle kick that complements the other flavors.
- Grind fresh black pepper on top to taste.
5. Serve:
- Serve immediately, allowing the prosciutto to showcase its delicate texture and the arugula to maintain its freshness.

Nutrition Information:
Note: Nutrition information is approximate and may vary based on specific ingredients used.
- Calories: 350 per serving
- Protein: 18g
- Fat: 28g
- Carbohydrates: 2g
- Fiber: 1g
- Sugar: 0g
- Sodium: 950mg
Indulge in the simplicity and sophistication of this Prosciutto, Pecorino & Arugula dish, a culinary masterpiece inspired by the renowned flavors of Tom Douglas's Serious Pie restaurant.

57. Buffalo Mozzarella with Tomato Sauce & Basil with Chili Flakes & Olive Oil

Indulge in the savory delights inspired by the menu of Tom Douglas's renowned Serious Pie restaurant with this exquisite recipe for Buffalo Mozzarella with Tomato Sauce & Basil, enhanced with a kick of Chili Flakes and the richness of Olive Oil. Elevate your dining experience with the perfect blend of fresh, high-quality ingredients that pay homage to the culinary excellence of Serious Pie.

Serving: Serves 4
Preparation Time: 15 minutes
Ready Time: 20 minutes

Ingredients:
- 1 pound fresh Buffalo Mozzarella, sliced
- 2 cups ripe tomatoes, diced
- 1/4 cup fresh basil leaves, torn
- 1 teaspoon red chili flakes (adjust to taste)
- 3 tablespoons extra-virgin olive oil
- Salt and pepper to taste

Instructions:
1. Prepare the Tomato Sauce:
- In a medium saucepan, heat 2 tablespoons of olive oil over medium heat.
- Add diced tomatoes and cook until they release their juices and the sauce thickens slightly, approximately 8-10 minutes.
- Season with salt and pepper to taste.
2. Assemble the Dish:
- Arrange the sliced Buffalo Mozzarella on a serving platter.
- Spoon the warm tomato sauce over the mozzarella slices, ensuring even coverage.
3. Enhance with Basil and Chili Flakes:
- Sprinkle torn basil leaves generously over the mozzarella and tomato sauce.
- For a hint of heat, evenly distribute red chili flakes over the dish.
4. Finish with Olive Oil:
- Drizzle the remaining tablespoon of olive oil over the top, adding a luscious richness to the ensemble.
5. Serve:
- Serve immediately while the mozzarella is still slightly warm, allowing the flavors to meld together.

Nutrition Information:
Note: Nutritional values are approximate and may vary based on specific ingredients used.

- Calories per serving: 300
- Total Fat: 22g
- Saturated Fat: 10g
- Trans Fat: 0g
- Cholesterol: 45mg
- Sodium: 400mg
- Total Carbohydrates: 5g
- Dietary Fiber: 1g
- Sugars: 3g
- Protein: 18g

Enjoy this exquisite Buffalo Mozzarella with Tomato Sauce & Basil creation, a tantalizing ode to the culinary mastery found at Tom Douglas's Serious Pie restaurant.

58. Soft Farm Egg, Guanciale & Grana Padano with Olive Oil & Chili Flakes

Indulge in the rustic charm of Tom Douglas's Serious Pie restaurant with this exquisite dish featuring Soft Farm Egg, Guanciale & Grana Padano, drizzled with extra virgin olive oil and a hint of chili flakes. The combination of velvety farm-fresh eggs, savory guanciale, and the rich, nutty notes of Grana Padano cheese creates a symphony of flavors that pays homage to the culinary mastery of Serious Pie.

Serving: This recipe serves 2.
Preparation Time: 15 minutes
Ready Time: 20 minutes

Ingredients:
- 4 farm-fresh eggs
- 100g guanciale, thinly sliced
- 50g Grana Padano cheese, shaved
- 2 tablespoons extra virgin olive oil
- 1/2 teaspoon chili flakes
- Salt and pepper to taste

Instructions:
1. Soft Farm Eggs:

- Bring a pot of water to a gentle simmer.
- Carefully crack the eggs into separate small bowls.
- Create a gentle whirlpool in the simmering water using a spoon and slide the eggs, one at a time, into the center of the whirlpool.
- Poach the eggs for 3-4 minutes until the whites are set but the yolks remain runny.
- Carefully remove the poached eggs with a slotted spoon and place them on a paper towel to drain excess water.
2. Crispy Guanciale:
- In a skillet over medium heat, cook the thinly sliced guanciale until it becomes crispy and golden brown.
- Transfer the guanciale to a plate lined with paper towels to absorb excess grease.
3. Assembly:
- Place the poached eggs on serving plates.
- Distribute the crispy guanciale around the eggs.
- Sprinkle shaved Grana Padano over the eggs and guanciale.
- Drizzle extra virgin olive oil over the dish.
- Sprinkle chili flakes for a hint of heat.
- Season with salt and pepper to taste.
4. Serve:
- Serve immediately, allowing the runny yolk to mingle with the guanciale, Grana Padano, and olive oil.

Nutrition Information:
(Per serving)
- Calories: 420 kcal
- Protein: 21g
- Fat: 34g
- Carbohydrates: 2g
- Fiber: 0.5g
- Sugar: 0g
- Sodium: 780mg
Elevate your home cooking with this sophisticated dish inspired by the culinary delights of Tom Douglas's Serious Pie. Enjoy the harmonious blend of textures and flavors that make this Soft Farm Egg, Guanciale & Grana Padano with Olive Oil & Chili Flakes a standout on any dining table.

59. Sweet Fennel Sausage with Roasted Red Pepper & Pecorino with Chili Flakes & Olive Oil

Indulge your taste buds in a symphony of flavors with this delectable recipe inspired by the menu of Tom Douglas's Serious Pie restaurant. The Sweet Fennel Sausage with Roasted Red Pepper & Pecorino, adorned with a sprinkle of chili flakes and a drizzle of olive oil, is a culinary masterpiece that combines the rich warmth of fennel sausage with the smoky sweetness of roasted red peppers and the bold kick of chili flakes. Topped with the distinctive nuttiness of Pecorino cheese, this dish is a celebration of savory and spicy notes that will transport you to the heart of Serious Pie's culinary experience.

Serving: 4 servings
Preparation Time: 15 minutes
Ready Time: 30 minutes

Ingredients:
- 1 lb sweet fennel sausage, casings removed
- 2 red bell peppers, roasted and thinly sliced
- 1 cup Pecorino cheese, shaved
- 1 teaspoon chili flakes (adjust to taste)
- 2 tablespoons olive oil
- Salt and black pepper to taste
- Fresh basil leaves for garnish (optional)

Instructions:
1. Preheat the Oven:
Preheat your oven to 400°F (200°C).
2. Roast Red Peppers:
Place the red bell peppers on a baking sheet and roast them in the preheated oven until the skins blister and turn black. Remove from the oven, let them cool, and then peel off the skins. Slice the roasted peppers thinly.
3. Cook the Sausage:
In a large skillet over medium heat, cook the sweet fennel sausage, breaking it apart with a spatula, until browned and cooked through. Remove excess fat if needed.
4. Combine Ingredients:

Add the roasted red pepper slices to the cooked sausage in the skillet. Toss them together until well combined. Season with salt and black pepper to taste.

5. Assemble and Garnish:

Transfer the sausage and pepper mixture to a serving dish. Sprinkle the shaved Pecorino cheese over the top, and then sprinkle with chili flakes. Drizzle the olive oil over the dish. Garnish with fresh basil leaves if desired.

6. Serve:

Serve the Sweet Fennel Sausage with Roasted Red Pepper & Pecorino hot, allowing the cheese to slightly melt over the savory sausage and peppers.

Nutrition Information:

Note: Nutrition information is approximate and may vary based on specific ingredients used.

- Calories: 450 per serving
- Total Fat: 35g
- Saturated Fat: 12g
- Cholesterol: 75mg
- Sodium: 1100mg
- Total Carbohydrates: 5g
- Dietary Fiber: 1g
- Sugars: 2g
- Protein: 25g

This dish not only captures the essence of Serious Pie's menu but also elevates your home-cooking experience with a burst of flavors that will leave your guests craving for more. Enjoy the Serious Pie magic in the comfort of your own kitchen!

60. Roasted Chanterelle Mushrooms with Truffle Cheese & Thyme with Chili Flakes & Olive Oil

Indulge your taste buds in a culinary journey inspired by the renowned Serious Pie restaurant, as we present a delectable creation straight from their menu. Roasted Chanterelle Mushrooms with Truffle Cheese & Thyme, elevated with a hint of Chili Flakes and Olive Oil, promises a symphony of flavors that dance on your palate. This dish is a celebration of earthy chanterelle mushrooms, rich truffle cheese, and the aromatic infusion of thyme, creating a sensational blend that echoes the sophistication of Tom Douglas's culinary expertise.

Serving: 4 servings
Preparation Time: 15 minutes
Ready Time: 35 minutes

Ingredients:
- 1 pound fresh chanterelle mushrooms, cleaned and trimmed
- 1 cup truffle cheese, grated
- 2 tablespoons fresh thyme leaves, chopped
- 1 teaspoon chili flakes (adjust to taste)
- 3 tablespoons olive oil
- Salt and pepper to taste

Instructions:
1. Preheat the Oven:
Preheat your oven to 400°F (200°C), ensuring it reaches the optimal temperature for roasting.
2. Prepare the Chanterelle Mushrooms:
Clean and trim the chanterelle mushrooms, ensuring they are free from any debris. If the mushrooms are large, consider slicing them into bite-sized pieces.
3. Create the Flavor Base:
In a mixing bowl, combine the cleaned chanterelle mushrooms with olive oil, fresh thyme leaves, chili flakes, salt, and pepper. Toss the ingredients together, ensuring the mushrooms are evenly coated with the flavorful mixture.
4. Roast to Perfection:
Spread the seasoned chanterelle mushrooms evenly on a baking sheet. Roast in the preheated oven for approximately 20-25 minutes or until the mushrooms are golden brown and have a delightful roasted aroma.
5. Cheesy Indulgence:
Once the mushrooms are roasted, sprinkle the grated truffle cheese over the top. Return the baking sheet to the oven and continue baking for an additional 5-7 minutes, or until the cheese is melted and bubbly.
6. Serve with Elegance:
Remove the roasted chanterelle mushrooms with truffle cheese from the oven. Allow them to cool for a few minutes before serving. Garnish with

additional fresh thyme leaves and chili flakes for a visual and flavorful appeal.

Nutrition Information:
Note: Nutritional values are approximate and may vary based on specific ingredients used.
- Calories: 280 per serving
- Total Fat: 20g
- Saturated Fat: 8g
- Trans Fat: 0g
- Cholesterol: 35mg
- Sodium: 450mg
- Total Carbohydrates: 15g
- Dietary Fiber: 3g
- Sugars: 2g
- Protein: 12g

Elevate your dining experience with this tantalizing recipe inspired by the culinary mastery of Tom Douglas's Serious Pie. Roasted Chanterelle Mushrooms with Truffle Cheese & Thyme is a dish that embodies the essence of sophistication and gastronomic delight.

61. Hazelnut Brown Butter Cake with Caramel Sauce & Whipped Cream

Indulge in the decadent world of Tom Douglas's Serious Pie with our Hazelnut Brown Butter Cake, a sublime dessert that captures the essence of sophistication and comfort. This recipe elevates the rich, nutty flavor of hazelnuts, complements it with the warmth of brown butter, and drizzles it with a luscious caramel sauce. Topped with billowy whipped cream, it's a symphony of flavors that will transport you to the heart of culinary excellence.

Serving: This recipe yields 10 servings.
Preparation Time: 30 minutes
Ready Time: 1 hour 30 minutes

Ingredients:
- 1 cup unsalted butter

- 1 cup all-purpose flour
- 1 cup hazelnuts, toasted and finely ground
- 1 cup granulated sugar
- 1 teaspoon baking powder
- 1/2 teaspoon salt
- 4 large eggs
- 1 teaspoon vanilla extract

For Caramel Sauce:
- 1 cup granulated sugar
- 1/4 cup water
- 1/2 cup heavy cream
- 2 tablespoons unsalted butter
- Pinch of salt

For Whipped Cream:
- 1 cup heavy cream
- 2 tablespoons powdered sugar
- 1 teaspoon vanilla extract

Instructions:
1. Preheat the oven to 350°F (175°C). Grease and flour a 9-inch round cake pan.
2. In a saucepan, melt the butter over medium heat, swirling occasionally until it turns golden brown and has a nutty aroma. Remove from heat and let it cool.
3. In a mixing bowl, combine the flour, ground hazelnuts, sugar, baking powder, and salt.
4. In a separate bowl, whisk together the eggs and vanilla extract. Gradually add the brown butter, stirring continuously.
5. Gently fold the wet ingredients into the dry ingredients until just combined. Pour the batter into the prepared cake pan.
6. Bake for 25-30 minutes or until a toothpick inserted into the center comes out clean. Allow the cake to cool in the pan for 10 minutes before transferring it to a wire rack.
7. While the cake is cooling, prepare the caramel sauce. In a saucepan, combine sugar and water over medium heat. Let it simmer without stirring until it turns a deep amber color. Remove from heat and carefully stir in the cream, butter, and salt. Allow it to cool.
8. For the whipped cream, beat the heavy cream, powdered sugar, and vanilla extract together until stiff peaks form.

9. Once the cake has cooled, drizzle the caramel sauce over the top and garnish with dollops of whipped cream.

Nutrition Information:
(Per serving)
- Calories: 420
- Total Fat: 28g
- Saturated Fat: 14g
- Cholesterol: 135mg
- Sodium: 190mg
- Total Carbohydrates: 38g
- Dietary Fiber: 2g
- Sugars: 28g
- Protein: 6g
Indulge in the exquisite flavors of this Hazelnut Brown Butter Cake, a dessert inspired by the culinary brilliance of Tom Douglas's Serious Pie.

62. Penn Cove Clams with Garlic, Chili Flakes & Lemon with Olive Oil & Basil

Indulge in the tantalizing flavors inspired by Tom Douglas's Serious Pie restaurant with our exquisite recipe for Penn Cove Clams with Garlic, Chili Flakes & Lemon, drizzled with Olive Oil & Basil. This dish captures the essence of the restaurant's commitment to fresh, high-quality ingredients and bold combinations. Elevate your culinary experience with this delightful seafood creation that marries the brininess of Penn Cove clams with the warmth of garlic, a hint of chili flakes, and the brightness of lemon, all tied together with the richness of olive oil and the freshness of basil.

Serving: 4 servings
Preparation Time: 15 minutes
Ready Time: 30 minutes

Ingredients:
- 2 pounds Penn Cove clams, scrubbed and cleaned
- 3 tablespoons olive oil
- 4 cloves garlic, finely minced

- 1 teaspoon chili flakes (adjust to taste)
- Zest of 1 lemon
- Juice of 1 lemon
- Salt and black pepper to taste
- Fresh basil leaves, thinly sliced, for garnish

Instructions:
1. Prepare the Clams: Rinse the Penn Cove clams under cold water, scrubbing away any grit or debris. Discard any clams with cracked shells or that do not close when tapped.
2. Sauté the Aromatics: In a large, deep skillet, heat the olive oil over medium heat. Add the minced garlic and chili flakes, sautéing until the garlic becomes fragrant and lightly golden.
3. Cook the Clams: Add the cleaned clams to the skillet, stirring to coat them in the garlic-infused oil. Pour in the lemon juice and sprinkle lemon zest over the clams. Season with salt and black pepper to taste.
4. Cover and Steam: Cover the skillet with a lid and let the clams steam for about 8-10 minutes or until they open. Discard any clams that do not open.
5. Finish with Basil: Once the clams have opened, remove the skillet from heat. Sprinkle fresh basil leaves over the clams and give everything a gentle toss to combine.
6. Serve: Transfer the Penn Cove Clams to a serving dish, drizzling any remaining pan juices over the top. Garnish with additional fresh basil leaves for a burst of color and flavor.

Nutrition Information:
(Note: Nutrition information is approximate and may vary based on specific ingredients and serving sizes.)
- Calories: 240 per serving
- Protein: 23g
- Fat: 11g
- Carbohydrates: 12g
- Fiber: 2g
- Sugars: 1g
- Sodium: 600mg

Embrace the essence of Serious Pie's culinary artistry with this delectable dish that balances the richness of clams with the vibrancy of garlic, lemon, and basil—a symphony of flavors that will transport your taste buds to new heights.

63. Finocchiona Salami, Castelvetrano Olives & Tomato with Chili Flakes & Olive Oil

Indulge your taste buds with a delightful creation inspired by the renowned Serious Pie restaurant by Tom Douglas. This exquisite dish features the savory allure of Finocchiona Salami, the buttery richness of Castelvetrano Olives, and the vibrant burst of tomatoes, all heightened by a tantalizing blend of chili flakes and olive oil. This recipe is a celebration of bold flavors and quality ingredients, a true reflection of the culinary excellence that defines Serious Pie.

Serving: Ideal for sharing, this dish serves 4.
Preparation Time: 20 minutes
Ready Time: 20 minutes

Ingredients:
- 1/2 lb Finocchiona Salami, thinly sliced
- 1 cup Castelvetrano Olives, pitted
- 1 cup cherry tomatoes, halved
- 1 teaspoon chili flakes (adjust to taste)
- 1/4 cup extra virgin olive oil

Instructions:
1. Prepare the Ingredients:
- Slice the Finocchiona Salami thinly.
- Pit the Castelvetrano Olives if they are not already pitted.
- Halve the cherry tomatoes.
2. Assemble the Dish:
- Arrange the Finocchiona Salami slices on a serving platter.
- Scatter the Castelvetrano Olives and cherry tomato halves over the salami.
3. Season with Chili Flakes:
- Sprinkle the chili flakes evenly over the salami, olives, and tomatoes. Adjust the amount according to your spice preference.
4. Drizzle with Olive Oil:

- Finish the dish by drizzling extra virgin olive oil over the entire platter. The high-quality olive oil enhances the flavors and adds a luxurious touch.
5. Serve and Enjoy:
- Present the dish to your guests, allowing them to appreciate the vibrant colors and enticing aromas. Serve with crusty bread or crackers for a complete experience.

Nutrition Information:
Note: Nutritional values are approximate and may vary based on specific ingredients used.
- Calories per serving: 320
- Protein: 18g
- Fat: 28g
- Carbohydrates: 6g
- Fiber: 2g
- Sugar: 2g
- Sodium: 1100mg
Indulge in the rich flavors of Finocchiona Salami, Castelvetrano Olives & Tomato with Chili Flakes & Olive Oil – a culinary masterpiece inspired by the innovation and taste expertise of Tom Douglas's Serious Pie. This dish promises to elevate your dining experience with every savory bite.

64. Buffalo Mozzarella, San Marzano Tomato & Basil with Chili Flakes & Olive Oil

Indulge in the culinary magic inspired by Tom Douglas's Serious Pie restaurant with this exquisite Buffalo Mozzarella, San Marzano Tomato & Basil dish. Elevating the classic flavors of Italy, this recipe brings together the creaminess of buffalo mozzarella, the sweetness of San Marzano tomatoes, and the aromatic touch of fresh basil. Enhanced with a hint of chili flakes and drizzled with extra virgin olive oil, this dish is a celebration of simplicity and sophistication. Recreate the signature taste of Serious Pie in your own kitchen and transport your taste buds to a world of culinary excellence.

Serving: 4 servings

Preparation Time: 15 minutes
Ready Time: 15 minutes

Ingredients:
- 1 pound buffalo mozzarella, sliced
- 4 large San Marzano tomatoes, sliced
- 1 cup fresh basil leaves
- 1 teaspoon chili flakes
- 4 tablespoons extra virgin olive oil
- Salt and black pepper to taste

Instructions:
1. Arrange the slices of buffalo mozzarella and San Marzano tomatoes on a serving platter, alternating them for an appealing presentation.
2. Sprinkle fresh basil leaves evenly over the mozzarella and tomatoes.
3. In a small bowl, combine chili flakes, salt, and black pepper. Sprinkle the mixture over the arranged ingredients.
4. Drizzle extra virgin olive oil generously over the entire dish, ensuring each element is lightly coated.
5. Allow the flavors to meld for a few minutes before serving to enhance the taste.
6. Serve the Buffalo Mozzarella, San Marzano Tomato & Basil with crusty bread or as a refreshing side dish to complement your meal.

Nutrition Information:
Note: Nutritional values are approximate and may vary based on specific ingredients and serving sizes.
- Calories per serving: 320
- Total Fat: 25g
- Saturated Fat: 12g
- Trans Fat: 0g
- Cholesterol: 50mg
- Sodium: 400mg
- Total Carbohydrates: 8g
- Dietary Fiber: 2g
- Sugars: 5g
- Protein: 18g

Immerse yourself in the essence of Tom Douglas's culinary expertise with this delightful dish, embodying the spirit of Serious Pie's commitment to exceptional flavors and quality ingredients.

65. Wild Mushrooms with Truffle Cheese with Chili Flakes & Olive Oil

Savor the earthy delight of wild mushrooms paired with the luxurious flavor of truffle cheese, elevated with a hint of heat from chili flakes and the richness of olive oil. Inspired by the renowned Serious Pie restaurant, this dish captures the essence of its rustic yet refined culinary ethos, bringing the forest's bounty to your table.

Serving: 2-4 servings
Preparation Time: 15 minutes
Ready Time: 25 minutes

Ingredients:
- 1 pound assorted wild mushrooms (such as chanterelles, porcini, shiitake), cleaned and sliced
- 2 tablespoons olive oil
- 2 cloves garlic, minced
- Salt and black pepper to taste
- 1/4 teaspoon chili flakes (adjust to taste)
- 4 ounces truffle cheese, thinly sliced or grated
- Fresh parsley, chopped (for garnish)

Instructions:
1. Prepare the Mushrooms: Heat 1 tablespoon of olive oil in a large skillet over medium-high heat. Add the mushrooms and sauté for 5-7 minutes until they start to brown and release their moisture.
2. Season and Flavor: Add minced garlic, salt, black pepper, and chili flakes to the mushrooms. Sauté for an additional 2-3 minutes, allowing the flavors to meld. Adjust seasoning to taste.
3. Melt the Cheese: Reduce the heat to medium-low. Layer the thinly sliced or grated truffle cheese over the mushrooms. Cover the skillet and let it cook for 3-5 minutes until the cheese melts and coats the mushrooms.
4. Finish and Garnish: Drizzle the remaining tablespoon of olive oil over the melted cheese and mushrooms. Garnish with freshly chopped parsley for a burst of freshness.

Nutrition Information (per serving, based on 4 servings):
- Calories: 240
- Total Fat: 18g
- Saturated Fat: 6g
- Trans Fat: 0g
- Cholesterol: 20mg
- Sodium: 300mg
- Total Carbohydrate: 12g
- Dietary Fiber: 3g
- Sugars: 3g
- Protein: 9g

Note: Nutrition information is approximate and may vary based on specific ingredients used.

This dish is best served hot, as soon as the cheese has melted over the savory mushrooms. Pair it with a crusty bread or as a side to a main course for a gourmet dining experience reminiscent of Serious Pie's culinary finesse.

66. Soft Farm Egg, Prosciutto, Arugula & Pecorino with Olive Oil & Chili Flakes

Indulge in the exquisite flavors of Tom Douglas's Serious Pie restaurant with this delectable dish featuring soft farm eggs, savory prosciutto, peppery arugula, and flavorful Pecorino cheese drizzled with olive oil and a hint of chili flakes. This dish embodies the restaurant's commitment to using fresh, high-quality ingredients and simple yet bold flavors.

Serving: 2 servings
Preparation time: 10 minutes
Ready time: 15 minutes

Ingredients:
- 4 large farm eggs
- 4 slices of prosciutto
- 2 cups arugula, washed and dried
- 1/4 cup shaved Pecorino cheese
- 2 tablespoons extra-virgin olive oil

114

- Pinch of chili flakes
- Salt and black pepper to taste

Instructions:
1. Prepare the Ingredients:
- Bring a pot of water to a gentle simmer. Carefully add the eggs and cook for 6-7 minutes for a soft, runny yolk. Remove the eggs with a slotted spoon and place them in a bowl of ice water for a minute before peeling. Set aside.
- Heat a skillet over medium heat. Place the prosciutto slices in the skillet and cook for 1-2 minutes on each side until lightly crispy. Remove from the skillet and set aside.
2. Assemble the Dish:
- Arrange a handful of arugula on each serving plate.
3. Prepare the Soft Farm Eggs:
- Carefully cut the top off each soft-boiled egg and gently place them on the arugula bed.
4. Add Prosciutto and Pecorino:
- Crumble or tear the crispy prosciutto over the eggs.
- Sprinkle the shaved Pecorino cheese on top.
5. Drizzle with Olive Oil and Chili Flakes:
- Drizzle extra-virgin olive oil over the dish.
- Sprinkle a pinch of chili flakes for a touch of heat.
6. Season and Serve:
- Season lightly with salt and freshly ground black pepper to taste.

Nutrition Information (per serving):
- Calories: Approximately 300
- Protein: 18g
- Fat: 23g
- Carbohydrates: 2g
- Fiber: 1g
- Sodium: 650mg
- Sugar: 1g
Note: Nutritional values are approximate and may vary depending on specific ingredients used.

67. Anchovy & Soft Farm Egg with Tomato Sauce & Chili Flakes with Olive Oil & Basil

This recipe draws inspiration from the vibrant flavors of Tom Douglas's Serious Pie restaurant. The combination of salty anchovies, creamy farm eggs, tangy tomato sauce, and the kick of chili flakes, all brought together with fragrant basil and olive oil, creates a harmonious dish that tantalizes the taste buds.

Serving: 2 servings
Preparation time: 10 minutes
Ready time: 20 minutes

Ingredients:
- 4 large eggs
- 1 can (2 ounces) anchovy fillets, drained and chopped
- 1 cup tomato sauce
- 1 teaspoon chili flakes (adjust to taste)
- 2 tablespoons olive oil
- Fresh basil leaves, for garnish
- Salt and pepper to taste

Instructions:
1. Prepare the Eggs:
- Bring a pot of water to a gentle simmer. Carefully add the eggs and cook for 6 minutes for soft-boiled eggs. Remove the eggs and transfer them to an ice water bath to stop the cooking process. Once cooled, carefully peel the eggs and set them aside.
2. Prepare the Sauce:
- In a saucepan, heat the olive oil over medium heat. Add the chopped anchovy fillets and cook for 1-2 minutes until they start to dissolve.
- Pour in the tomato sauce and add chili flakes. Stir well and let it simmer for about 5-7 minutes, allowing the flavors to meld. Season with salt and pepper to taste.
3. Assemble:
- Place a generous spoonful of the tomato and anchovy sauce onto each serving plate.
- Gently slice the soft-boiled eggs in half and arrange them on top of the sauce.

- Drizzle a little extra olive oil over the eggs and sauce.
4. Garnish:
- Tear fresh basil leaves and sprinkle them over the dish for a burst of fragrance and color.
- Optionally, add a sprinkle of additional chili flakes for extra heat.
5. Serve:
- Serve immediately, allowing guests to mix the egg yolk with the tomato sauce for a delightful blend of flavors.

Nutrition Information (approximate values per serving):
- Calories: 320
- Fat: 24g
- Carbohydrates: 8g
- Protein: 18g
- Fiber: 2g
Enjoy this flavorful dish as a brunch option or a delightful appetizer that showcases the unique tastes of Serious Pie's menu.

68. Smoked Provolone, Tomato Sauce & Sweet Fennel Sausage with Chili Flakes & Olive Oil & Basil

Indulge in the savory symphony inspired by the renowned Serious Pie restaurant. This recipe captures the essence of their culinary mastery, featuring Smoked Provolone, Tomato Sauce & Sweet Fennel Sausage with a kick of Chili Flakes, drizzled with Olive Oil, and garnished with fresh Basil. Elevate your pizza experience with this tantalizing combination that marries tradition with innovation.

Serving: 4 servings
Preparation Time: 20 minutes
Ready Time: 30 minutes

Ingredients:
- 1 lb pizza dough (store-bought or homemade)
- 1 cup tomato sauce
- 1 cup smoked provolone, shredded
- 1 cup sweet fennel sausage, cooked and crumbled

- 1 teaspoon chili flakes (adjust to taste)
- 2 tablespoons olive oil
- Fresh basil leaves for garnish

Instructions:
1. Preheat the Oven:
Preheat your oven to 475°F (245°C). If you have a pizza stone, place it in the oven during preheating.
2. Prepare the Dough:
Roll out the pizza dough on a floured surface to your desired thickness. If you have a pizza peel, transfer the dough onto it. If not, you can use parchment paper on a baking sheet.
3. Assemble the Pizza:
Spread a generous layer of tomato sauce over the rolled-out dough, leaving a small border for the crust. Evenly distribute the smoked provolone and crumbled sweet fennel sausage over the sauce. Sprinkle chili flakes for that extra kick.
4. Bake in the Oven:
If using a pizza stone, carefully transfer the pizza onto the preheated stone in the oven. If using a baking sheet, place the sheet in the oven. Bake for about 12-15 minutes or until the crust is golden and the cheese is bubbly and slightly browned.
5. Drizzle with Olive Oil:
Once out of the oven, drizzle the hot pizza with olive oil for added richness and flavor.
6. Garnish with Fresh Basil:
Scatter fresh basil leaves over the pizza for a burst of herbal freshness.
7. Slice and Serve:
Allow the pizza to cool for a few minutes before slicing. Serve hot and enjoy the delicious blend of flavors.

Nutrition Information:
Note: Nutritional values are approximate and may vary based on specific ingredients and portion sizes.
- Calories per serving: 450 kcal
- Total Fat: 20g
- Saturated Fat: 7g
- Trans Fat: 0g
- Cholesterol: 40mg
- Sodium: 900mg

- Total Carbohydrates: 50g
- Dietary Fiber: 3g
- Sugars: 5g
- Protein: 18g

Indulge in the savory pleasure of Smoked Provolone, Tomato Sauce & Sweet Fennel Sausage Pizza, a delightful homage to the culinary artistry of Serious Pie.

69. Guanciale, Castelvetrano Olives & Tomato Sauce with Chili Flakes & Olive Oil & Basil

Experience the bold and authentic flavors of Serious Pie's renowned cuisine with this exquisite recipe inspired by the innovative menu of Tom Douglas. Guanciale, Castelvetrano Olives & Tomato Sauce with Chili Flakes & Olive Oil & Basil captures the essence of the restaurant's commitment to quality ingredients and creative combinations. This dish is a delightful symphony of rich guanciale, briny Castelvetrano olives, vibrant tomato sauce, and the subtle heat of chili flakes, all brought together with the freshness of olive oil and basil. Prepare to embark on a culinary journey that mirrors the sophistication and deliciousness of Serious Pie's offerings.

Serving: 4 servings
Preparation Time: 15 minutes
Ready Time: 45 minutes

Ingredients:
- 1 pound pasta of your choice
- 1/4 cup extra-virgin olive oil
- 1/2 cup guanciale, thinly sliced
- 1 cup Castelvetrano olives, pitted and halved
- 2 cups tomato sauce (homemade or store-bought)
- 1 teaspoon red chili flakes (adjust to taste)
- Salt and black pepper to taste
- Fresh basil leaves for garnish

Instructions:

1. Cook the pasta according to package instructions until al dente. Drain and set aside.
2. In a large skillet, heat the olive oil over medium heat. Add the guanciale and sauté until golden and crispy.
3. Add the halved Castelvetrano olives to the skillet, stirring to combine with the guanciale.
4. Pour in the tomato sauce, stirring well to incorporate. Allow the mixture to simmer for 10-15 minutes, allowing the flavors to meld.
5. Sprinkle in the red chili flakes, salt, and black pepper, adjusting the seasoning to your liking.
6. Add the cooked pasta to the skillet, tossing to coat it evenly with the sauce. Cook for an additional 5 minutes, ensuring the pasta absorbs the flavors.
7. Remove the skillet from heat and drizzle with additional olive oil for a finishing touch.
8. Serve the pasta in individual bowls, garnished with fresh basil leaves.

Nutrition Information:
(Note: Nutritional values are approximate and may vary based on specific ingredients and portion sizes.)
- Calories: 450 per serving
- Protein: 12g
- Fat: 18g
- Carbohydrates: 60g
- Fiber: 5g
- Sugar: 8g
- Sodium: 800mg
Elevate your home cooking with this delightful dish that pays homage to the culinary brilliance of Tom Douglas's Serious Pie.

70. Yukon Gold Potato, Rosemary & Caciocavallo with Olive Oil & Chili Flakes & Basil

Elevate your culinary experience with this inspired recipe from Tom Douglas's Serious Pie restaurant. The marriage of Yukon Gold potatoes, fragrant rosemary, rich Caciocavallo cheese, and the warmth of olive oil and chili flakes creates a dish that is both comforting and sophisticated.

Topped with fresh basil, each bite is a symphony of flavors that pays homage to the restaurant's commitment to serious, quality pies.

Serving: 4 servings
Preparation Time: 15 minutes
Ready Time: 45 minutes

Ingredients:
- 4 large Yukon Gold potatoes, washed and thinly sliced
- 2 tablespoons fresh rosemary, finely chopped
- 1 cup Caciocavallo cheese, shredded
- 1/4 cup extra-virgin olive oil
- 1 teaspoon chili flakes (adjust to taste)
- Salt and pepper to taste
- Fresh basil leaves for garnish

Instructions:
1. Preheat the oven to 400°F (200°C).
2. In a large bowl, toss the thinly sliced Yukon Gold potatoes with rosemary, salt, and pepper until well combined.
3. Drizzle half of the olive oil over the bottom of a baking dish, spreading it evenly.
4. Arrange a layer of seasoned potato slices in the baking dish, ensuring even coverage.
5. Sprinkle a portion of the shredded Caciocavallo cheese over the potatoes.
6. Repeat the layering process until all the potatoes and cheese are used, finishing with a layer of potatoes on top.
7. Drizzle the remaining olive oil over the top layer and sprinkle chili flakes for a hint of heat.
8. Cover the baking dish with aluminum foil and bake for 30 minutes.
9. Remove the foil and continue baking for an additional 15 minutes or until the potatoes are tender and the top is golden brown.
10. Garnish with fresh basil leaves before serving.

Nutrition Information:
Note: Nutritional values are approximate and may vary based on specific ingredients used.
- Calories per serving: 320 kcal
- Total Fat: 15g

- Saturated Fat: 7g
- Trans Fat: 0g
- Cholesterol: 30mg
- Sodium: 250mg
- Total Carbohydrates: 40g
- Dietary Fiber: 5g
- Sugars: 2g
- Protein: 10g

Elevate your dining experience with this exquisite Yukon Gold Potato, Rosemary & Caciocavallo dish – a slice of Serious Pie's culinary artistry in the comfort of your own home.

71. Penn Cove Clams with House Pancetta & Lemon with Chili Flakes & Olive Oil & Basil

Indulge in the exquisite flavors of the Pacific Northwest with this inspired dish from Tom Douglas's Serious Pie restaurant. The Penn Cove Clams with House Pancetta & Lemon, enhanced with a hint of Chili Flakes, Olive Oil, and Basil, offer a symphony of tastes that will transport you straight to the heart of Seattle. The combination of fresh, locally-sourced ingredients and expert culinary craftsmanship makes this dish a standout on the menu.

Serving: Ideal for a delightful dinner for two or as an impressive appetizer for a gathering of friends. This recipe serves 4.
Preparation Time: 20 minutes
Ready Time: 30 minutes

Ingredients:
- 2 pounds Penn Cove clams, scrubbed clean
- 1/2 cup house pancetta, diced
- Zest of 1 lemon
- 1 teaspoon chili flakes (adjust to taste)
- 3 tablespoons extra virgin olive oil
- 1/4 cup fresh basil leaves, torn
- Salt and black pepper to taste

Instructions:

1. Prepare the Clams:
- Rinse the Penn Cove clams thoroughly under cold water to remove any sand or debris.
- Discard any clams with broken shells or that do not close when tapped.
2. Cook the Pancetta:
- In a large skillet over medium heat, cook the diced house pancetta until it becomes crispy and golden brown. Remove excess fat, leaving about a tablespoon in the pan.
3. Sauté the Clams:
- Add the cleaned clams to the skillet with pancetta. Stir gently to coat the clams in the rendered pancetta fat.
4. Seasoning:
- Sprinkle chili flakes over the clams, add the lemon zest, and season with salt and black pepper. Toss the ingredients to combine.
5. Steam the Clams:
- Pour the olive oil over the clams and cover the skillet. Allow the clams to steam for 5-7 minutes or until they open. Discard any clams that do not open.
6. Finish with Basil:
- Once the clams are cooked, toss in the torn basil leaves. Give it a final gentle stir to incorporate the flavors.
7. Serve:
- Transfer the clams and pancetta mixture to a serving platter. Drizzle with additional olive oil if desired. Serve immediately.

Nutrition Information:
(Per Serving - 1/4 of the recipe)
- Calories: 320 kcal
- Protein: 20g
- Fat: 18g
- Carbohydrates: 12g
- Fiber: 2g
- Sugar: 1g
- Sodium: 700mg

Enjoy the rich and savory experience of Penn Cove Clams with House Pancetta & Lemon, a culinary masterpiece that captures the essence of Tom Douglas's Serious Pie restaurant in every bite.

72. Prosciutto, Pecorino & Arugula with Olive Oil & Chili Flakes & Basil

Indulge in the delectable flavors inspired by Tom Douglas's Serious Pie restaurant with this elegant yet simple dish—Prosciutto, Pecorino & Arugula with Olive Oil & Chili Flakes & Basil. This appetizer perfectly balances the salty richness of prosciutto with the nutty notes of Pecorino, complemented by the peppery arugula and the warmth of chili flakes. Finished with a drizzle of high-quality olive oil and fresh basil, it's a symphony of flavors that will transport your taste buds to the heart of Serious Pie's culinary experience.

Serving: Ideal as a shared appetizer, this dish serves 4.
Preparation Time: 15 minutes
Ready Time: 15 minutes

Ingredients:
- 8 slices of prosciutto
- 1 cup arugula, washed and dried
- 1 cup Pecorino cheese, shaved
- 2 tablespoons high-quality olive oil
- 1 teaspoon chili flakes (adjust to taste)
- Fresh basil leaves for garnish

Instructions:
1. Prepare the Ingredients:
- Lay out the prosciutto slices on a serving platter.
- Wash and dry the arugula thoroughly.
- Shave the Pecorino cheese into thin slices.
2. Assemble the Dish:
- Place a few arugula leaves on each slice of prosciutto.
- Scatter Pecorino shavings over the arugula.
- Drizzle olive oil over the top, ensuring even coverage.
- Sprinkle chili flakes to add a hint of heat.
3. Garnish and Serve:
- Garnish the dish with fresh basil leaves for a burst of fragrance.
- Serve immediately to enjoy the vibrant flavors and textures.

Nutrition Information:

- *(Note: Nutritional values are approximate and may vary based on specific ingredients and portion sizes.)*
- Calories: 180 per serving
- Protein: 10g
- Carbohydrates: 2g
- Fat: 15g
- Saturated Fat: 6g
- Cholesterol: 30mg
- Sodium: 600mg
- Fiber: 1g
- Sugar: 0g

Indulge in the luxurious simplicity of this Prosciutto, Pecorino & Arugula dish, and savor the essence of Tom Douglas's Serious Pie right in your own home.

73. Buffalo Mozzarella with Tomato Sauce & Basil with Chili Flakes & Olive Oil & Basil

Indulge in the tantalizing flavors inspired by Tom Douglas's renowned Serious Pie restaurant with our Buffalo Mozzarella with Tomato Sauce & Basil, enhanced with a kick of Chili Flakes, drizzled in Olive Oil, and garnished with fresh Basil. This dish is a celebration of simplicity and quality ingredients, capturing the essence of Serious Pie's commitment to exquisite culinary experiences.

Serving: Serves 4
Preparation Time: 15 minutes
Ready Time: 20 minutes

Ingredients:
- 2 balls of Buffalo Mozzarella
- 2 cups tomato sauce (homemade or high-quality store-bought)
- 1 cup fresh basil leaves, torn
- 1 teaspoon chili flakes (adjust to taste)
- 2 tablespoons extra virgin olive oil
- Salt and pepper to taste

Instructions:

1. Preheat your oven to 375°F (190°C).
2. Slice the Buffalo Mozzarella into 1/4-inch thick rounds and set aside.
3. In a saucepan, heat the tomato sauce over medium heat until warmed through. Season with salt and pepper to taste.
4. On a baking sheet, arrange the Buffalo Mozzarella slices. Spoon a generous amount of warm tomato sauce over each slice.
5. Sprinkle chili flakes evenly over the mozzarella and tomato sauce.
6. Place the baking sheet in the preheated oven and bake for 10-12 minutes, or until the cheese is melted and bubbly.
7. Remove from the oven and drizzle extra virgin olive oil over the mozzarella and tomato slices.
8. Garnish with torn fresh basil leaves, distributing them evenly.
9. Serve the Buffalo Mozzarella with Tomato Sauce & Basil immediately, allowing the richness of the cheese and the freshness of the basil to shine.

Nutrition Information:
Note: Nutritional values are approximate and may vary based on specific ingredients used.
- Calories: 280 per serving
- Fat: 20g
- Saturated Fat: 8g
- Cholesterol: 45mg
- Sodium: 680mg
- Carbohydrates: 10g
- Fiber: 2g
- Sugars: 6g
- Protein: 15g
This Buffalo Mozzarella with Tomato Sauce & Basil dish is a delightful combination of creamy, savory, and slightly spicy elements that will transport you to the culinary world of Tom Douglas's Serious Pie. Enjoy the art of simple yet exquisite flavors at your own table.

74. Soft Farm Egg, Guanciale & Grana Padano with Olive Oil & Chili Flakes & Basil

Indulge in the exquisite flavors inspired by Tom Douglas's renowned Serious Pie restaurant with our Soft Farm Egg, Guanciale & Grana

Padano creation. This delightful dish combines the rich creaminess of soft farm eggs with the savory kick of guanciale, the bold nuttiness of Grana Padano, and the aromatic blend of olive oil, chili flakes, and fresh basil. Elevate your dining experience with this sophisticated yet comforting recipe that captures the essence of Serious Pie's culinary mastery.

Serving: 2 servings
Preparation Time: 15 minutes
Ready Time: 20 minutes

Ingredients:
- 4 large farm eggs
- 100g guanciale, thinly sliced
- 50g Grana Padano, shaved
- 2 tablespoons extra virgin olive oil
- 1/2 teaspoon chili flakes (adjust to taste)
- Fresh basil leaves for garnish
- Salt and pepper to taste

Instructions:
1. Preheat the Oven:
- Preheat your oven to 375°F (190°C).
2. Prepare Guanciale:
- In a skillet over medium heat, cook the guanciale slices until they become crispy. Remove from heat and set aside.
3. Soft Farm Eggs:
- Carefully crack the farm eggs into individual small bowls, ensuring the yolks remain intact.
4. Bake the Eggs:
- Grease two oven-safe ramekins with a bit of olive oil. Gently pour two eggs into each ramekin. Place the ramekins in the preheated oven and bake for about 8-10 minutes, or until the egg whites are set but the yolks are still runny.
5. Assemble:
- Sprinkle the crispy guanciale over the baked eggs. Add shaved Grana Padano on top. Drizzle with extra virgin olive oil and sprinkle chili flakes. Season with salt and pepper to taste.
6. Garnish:
- Garnish with fresh basil leaves for a burst of aromatic freshness.

7. Serve:
- Serve immediately, allowing the creamy yolk to mix with the guanciale, Grana Padano, and the flavorful olive oil.

Nutrition Information:
- *(Per Serving)*
- Calories: 380
- Total Fat: 28g
- Saturated Fat: 8g
- Trans Fat: 0g
- Cholesterol: 390mg
- Sodium: 560mg
- Total Carbohydrates: 2g
- Dietary Fiber: 0g
- Sugars: 0g
- Protein: 27g

Elevate your home cooking with this Soft Farm Egg, Guanciale & Grana Padano masterpiece—a tantalizing blend of flavors that mirrors the culinary excellence of Serious Pie.

75. Sweet Fennel Sausage with Roasted Red Pepper & Pecorino with Chili Flakes & Olive Oil & Basil

Indulge your taste buds in a symphony of flavors with this delectable recipe inspired by the innovative menu of Tom Douglas's Serious Pie restaurant. Sweet Fennel Sausage with Roasted Red Pepper & Pecorino, enhanced with a kick of Chili Flakes, the richness of Olive Oil, and the freshness of Basil, creates a culinary masterpiece that tantalizes the senses. This dish perfectly captures the essence of Serious Pie's commitment to bold and imaginative combinations.

Serving: 4 servings
Preparation Time: 15 minutes
Ready Time: 45 minutes

Ingredients:
- 1 lb sweet fennel sausage, casings removed
- 2 red bell peppers, roasted and sliced

- 1 cup Pecorino Romano cheese, shaved
- 1 teaspoon chili flakes (adjust to taste)
- 3 tablespoons extra virgin olive oil
- Fresh basil leaves, for garnish
- Salt and black pepper to taste

Instructions:
1. Preheat the Oven:
Preheat your oven to 400°F (200°C).
2. Roast Red Peppers:
Place the red bell peppers on a baking sheet and roast in the preheated oven for about 20-25 minutes or until the skins are charred. Remove from the oven, place in a bowl, and cover with plastic wrap. Let them steam for 10 minutes, then peel off the skins, remove the seeds, and slice the peppers into strips.
3. Cook the Sausage:
In a large skillet over medium heat, cook the sweet fennel sausage, breaking it into crumbles with a spoon. Cook until browned and cooked through. Remove any excess grease.
4. Combine Ingredients:
Add the roasted red pepper strips to the skillet with the cooked sausage. Toss together until well combined. Season with salt and black pepper to taste.
5. Add Chili Flakes and Olive Oil:
Sprinkle chili flakes over the sausage and pepper mixture. Drizzle with extra virgin olive oil. Stir well to coat everything evenly.
6. Serve with Pecorino and Basil:
Transfer the sausage and pepper mixture to a serving platter. Sprinkle generously with shaved Pecorino Romano cheese. Garnish with fresh basil leaves.
7. Final Touch:
For an extra burst of flavor, finish the dish with an additional drizzle of olive oil and a pinch of chili flakes.

Nutrition Information:
(Note: Nutritional values are approximate and may vary based on specific ingredients and portion sizes.)
- Calories: 450 per serving
- Protein: 22g
- Carbohydrates: 5g

- Fat: 38g
- Fiber: 2g

Elevate your home cooking with this Serious Pie-inspired creation, where the sweet fennel sausage, roasted red peppers, and the richness of Pecorino come together to create a memorable dish that's perfect for any occasion.

76. Roasted Chanterelle Mushrooms with Truffle Cheese & Thyme with Chili Flakes & Olive Oil & Basil

Indulge your senses in the exquisite flavors of Roasted Chanterelle Mushrooms with Truffle Cheese & Thyme, elevated with a hint of Chili Flakes, Olive Oil, and fresh Basil. This recipe draws inspiration from the culinary brilliance of Tom Douglas's Serious Pie restaurant, where every dish is a symphony of taste and texture. The earthy aroma of chanterelle mushrooms, the decadence of truffle cheese, and the herbaceous notes of thyme come together in a harmonious union, creating a dish that's both comforting and sophisticated.

Serving: 4 servings
Preparation Time: 15 minutes
Ready Time: 30 minutes

Ingredients:
- 1 pound chanterelle mushrooms, cleaned and halved
- 1/2 cup truffle cheese, shaved or grated
- 2 tablespoons olive oil
- 1 teaspoon chili flakes (adjust to taste)
- 1 tablespoon fresh thyme leaves
- Salt and pepper to taste
- Fresh basil leaves for garnish

Instructions:
1. Preheat the Oven: Preheat your oven to 400°F (200°C).
2. Prepare the Chanterelle Mushrooms: Clean the chanterelle mushrooms thoroughly and cut them in half. Place them in a large mixing bowl.

3. Season the Mushrooms: Drizzle the chanterelle mushrooms with olive oil and sprinkle chili flakes, fresh thyme leaves, salt, and pepper. Toss well to ensure even coating.

4. Roast the Mushrooms: Spread the seasoned mushrooms on a baking sheet in a single layer. Roast in the preheated oven for about 20-25 minutes or until the mushrooms are golden brown and slightly crispy at the edges.

5. Add Truffle Cheese: About 5 minutes before the mushrooms are done, sprinkle the shaved or grated truffle cheese over the top. Allow it to melt and become gooey.

6. Finish with Basil: Once out of the oven, garnish the dish with fresh basil leaves for a burst of aromatic freshness.

7. Serve: Plate the roasted chanterelle mushrooms with truffle cheese & thyme immediately, and savor the symphony of flavors. Pair it with crusty bread or serve it as a side dish to complement your main course.

Nutrition Information:
Note: Nutritional values are approximate and may vary based on specific ingredients used.
- Calories: 180 per serving
- Protein: 8g
- Fat: 12g
- Carbohydrates: 15g
- Fiber: 3g
- Sugar: 2g
- Sodium: 300mg

Elevate your dining experience with this exquisite dish that captures the essence of Serious Pie's innovative menu. Roasted Chanterelle Mushrooms with Truffle Cheese & Thyme is a celebration of earthy, savory, and spicy notes that will leave your taste buds craving for more.

77. Hazelnut Brown Butter Cake with Caramel Sauce & Whipped Cream & Hazelnuts

Indulge in the rich flavors of Tom Douglas's Serious Pie with this delightful Hazelnut Brown Butter Cake, adorned with a luscious caramel sauce, fluffy whipped cream, and crunchy hazelnuts. This dessert captures the essence of the renowned restaurant's commitment to elevating simple ingredients into extraordinary culinary experiences. The nutty aroma of hazelnuts combined with the decadent brown butter creates a heavenly treat that will tantalize your taste buds and leave you craving more.

Serving: Serves: 8-10
Slice the cake and drizzle generously with caramel sauce. Top with a dollop of whipped cream and sprinkle crushed hazelnuts for a delightful finishing touch.
Preparation Time: 20 minutes
Ready Time: 1 hour 30 minutes

Ingredients:
For the Hazelnut Brown Butter Cake:
- 1 cup unsalted butter
- 1 cup all-purpose flour
- 1 cup hazelnut meal (ground hazelnuts)
- 1 teaspoon baking powder
- 1/2 teaspoon salt
- 1 cup granulated sugar
- 4 large eggs
- 1 teaspoon pure vanilla extract
- 1/2 cup whole milk
For the Caramel Sauce:
- 1 cup granulated sugar
- 6 tablespoons unsalted butter, cubed
- 1/2 cup heavy cream
- Pinch of salt
For the Whipped Cream & Garnish:
- 1 cup heavy cream
- 2 tablespoons powdered sugar
- 1/2 teaspoon pure vanilla extract
- 1/4 cup chopped hazelnuts, toasted

Instructions:
1. Preheat your oven to 350°F (175°C). Grease and flour a 9-inch round cake pan.
2. Begin by preparing the hazelnut brown butter. In a saucepan over medium heat, melt the butter. Continue cooking, stirring occasionally

until the butter turns a deep golden brown color and emits a nutty aroma. Remove from heat and let it cool slightly.

3. In a mixing bowl, sift together the flour, hazelnut meal, baking powder, and salt.

4. In a separate large bowl, whisk together the granulated sugar and eggs until pale and fluffy. Stir in the vanilla extract.

5. Slowly pour the brown butter into the egg mixture while whisking continuously until well combined.

6. Gradually add the dry ingredients to the wet ingredients, alternating with the milk, and gently fold until just combined. Do not overmix.

7. Pour the batter into the prepared cake pan and smooth the top. Bake in the preheated oven for 25-30 minutes or until a toothpick inserted into the center comes out clean.

8. While the cake is baking, prepare the caramel sauce. In a saucepan over medium heat, melt the granulated sugar. Once melted and amber in color, add the cubed butter and stir until fully incorporated. Slowly pour in the heavy cream while stirring continuously. Add a pinch of salt and simmer for 1-2 minutes until the sauce thickens slightly. Remove from heat and let it cool.

9. In a chilled mixing bowl, whip the heavy cream until soft peaks form. Add powdered sugar and vanilla extract, continue whipping until stiff peaks form.

10. Once the cake has cooled, slice it into servings. Drizzle each slice generously with the caramel sauce, add a dollop of whipped cream, and sprinkle with chopped toasted hazelnuts.

Nutrition Information (per serving, based on 8 servings, approximate):

- Calories: 550
- Total Fat: 38g
- Saturated Fat: 21g
- Trans Fat: 0g
- Cholesterol: 170mg
- Sodium: 290mg
- Total Carbohydrate: 49g
- Dietary Fiber: 2g
- Sugars: 36g
- Protein: 7g

Note: Nutrition information may vary based on specific ingredients and serving sizes used.

78. Penn Cove Clams with Garlic, Chili Flakes & Lemon with Olive Oil & Basil & Parsley

Penn Cove Clams with Garlic, Chili Flakes & Lemon with Olive Oil & Basil & Parsley is a delectable dish inspired by the flavors of Tom Douglas's Serious Pie restaurant. This recipe captures the essence of fresh seafood combined with vibrant herbs and spices, creating a flavorful and aromatic dish that delights the senses.

Serving: 2-4 servings
Preparation time: 15 minutes
Ready time: 25 minutes

Ingredients:
- 2 pounds Penn Cove clams, cleaned and scrubbed
- 3 tablespoons extra-virgin olive oil
- 4 cloves garlic, thinly sliced
- 1 teaspoon chili flakes (adjust to taste)
- Zest of 1 lemon
- Juice of 1 lemon
- Salt and freshly ground black pepper to taste
- 2 tablespoons fresh basil, chopped
- 2 tablespoons fresh parsley, chopped

Instructions:
1. Preparation: Rinse the Penn Cove clams thoroughly under cold water to remove any grit or sand. Scrub the shells gently if needed. Set aside.
2. Heat Olive Oil: In a large, deep skillet or pot over medium heat, add the olive oil. Once hot, add the sliced garlic and chili flakes. Sauté for 1-2 minutes until the garlic turns fragrant and slightly golden.
3. Add Clams: Increase the heat to medium-high. Add the cleaned clams to the skillet. Toss them gently to coat them with the garlic-infused oil. Sprinkle with lemon zest and season with salt and black pepper.
4. Cover and Cook: Cover the skillet or pot with a lid. Allow the clams to cook for about 5-7 minutes, shaking the pan occasionally. The clams should open up when cooked. Discard any clams that do not open.

5. Finish and Serve: Once the clams have opened, remove the skillet from heat. Squeeze fresh lemon juice over the clams and toss them gently. Sprinkle with chopped basil and parsley.
6. Plate and Garnish: Transfer the cooked clams to a serving dish, pouring any remaining juices from the skillet over the top. Garnish with additional fresh herbs if desired.

Nutrition Information: *(Per serving, based on 4 servings)*
- Calories: Approximately 235 kcal
- Fat: 12g
- Carbohydrates: 7g
- Protein: 23g
- Fiber: 1g
Note: Nutritional values are approximate and may vary based on specific ingredients used.
Tip: Serve this dish with crusty bread to soak up the flavorful broth. It pairs wonderfully with a glass of white wine for a delightful dining experience.

79. Finocchiona Salami, Castelvetrano Olives & Tomato with Chili Flakes & Olive Oil & Basil

This flavorful dish draws inspiration from the rustic yet sophisticated menu offerings at Tom Douglas's renowned Serious Pie restaurant. The combination of aromatic Finocchiona salami, briny Castelvetrano olives, vibrant tomatoes, and the subtle kick of chili flakes, olive oil, and fresh basil creates a tantalizing ensemble that captures the essence of Italian flavors in each bite.

Serving: 4 servings
Preparation time: 15 minutes
Ready time: 15 minutes

Ingredients:
- 1/2 lb Finocchiona salami, thinly sliced
- 1 cup Castelvetrano olives, pitted and halved
- 2 cups cherry tomatoes, halved
- 1 teaspoon chili flakes

- 4 tablespoons extra-virgin olive oil
- Fresh basil leaves, for garnish
- Salt and pepper to taste

Instructions:
1. Prepare the Ingredients:
- Thinly slice the Finocchiona salami and set it aside.
- Pit the Castelvetrano olives and cut them in halves.
- Halve the cherry tomatoes and set them aside.
2. Combine the Ingredients:
- In a mixing bowl, combine the sliced Finocchiona salami, halved Castelvetrano olives, and cherry tomatoes.
3. Season the Mixture:
- Sprinkle the chili flakes over the mixture for a subtle but spicy kick.
- Drizzle the extra-virgin olive oil generously over the ingredients.
- Season with salt and pepper to taste. Toss gently to coat everything evenly.
4. Assemble and Garnish:
- Arrange the mixture on a serving platter or individual plates.
- Garnish the dish with fresh basil leaves for a pop of color and added fragrance.
5. Serve and Enjoy:
- This dish is ready to be served immediately. Serve it as an appetizer or as a side dish alongside crusty bread or focaccia.

Nutrition Information (approximate values per serving):
- Calories: 320 kcal
- Total Fat: 28g
- Saturated Fat: 8g
- Cholesterol: 40mg
- Sodium: 900mg
- Total Carbohydrate: 6g
- Dietary Fiber: 2g
- Sugars: 2g
- Protein: 12g
Note: Nutritional values are approximate and can vary based on specific ingredients used and portion sizes.

80. Buffalo Mozzarella, San Marzano Tomato & Basil with Chili Flakes & Olive Oil & Basil

Experience the rustic elegance of Tom Douglas's Serious Pie restaurant with this delightful dish featuring the classic trio of Buffalo Mozzarella, San Marzano Tomatoes, and fresh Basil. The addition of chili flakes provides a subtle kick, while a drizzle of olive oil adds richness to the ensemble. Perfect for a casual gathering or a sophisticated dinner, this recipe captures the essence of Serious Pie's culinary mastery.

Serving: 4 servings
Preparation Time: 15 minutes
Ready Time: 15 minutes

Ingredients:
- 8 ounces Buffalo Mozzarella, sliced
- 1 pound San Marzano Tomatoes, sliced
- 1 bunch fresh Basil leaves
- 1 teaspoon chili flakes (adjust to taste)
- 2 tablespoons extra virgin olive oil
- Salt and black pepper to taste

Instructions:
1. Preheat your oven to 375°F (190°C).
2. Arrange the sliced Buffalo Mozzarella and San Marzano Tomatoes on a baking sheet, alternating them for an attractive presentation.
3. Sprinkle the fresh Basil leaves evenly over the cheese and tomatoes.
4. Sprinkle chili flakes over the top, adjusting the quantity based on your desired level of spiciness.
5. Season with salt and black pepper to taste.
6. Drizzle the extra virgin olive oil over the entire arrangement.
7. Place the baking sheet in the preheated oven and bake for 10-12 minutes or until the cheese is melted and bubbly.
8. Remove from the oven and let it rest for a couple of minutes before serving.
9. Optionally, garnish with additional fresh basil leaves and a dash of olive oil before serving.

Nutrition Information:

Note: Nutrition information is approximate and may vary based on specific ingredients used.
- Calories: 250 per serving
- Total Fat: 20g
- Saturated Fat: 8g
- Trans Fat: 0g
- Cholesterol: 40mg
- Sodium: 300mg
- Total Carbohydrates: 5g
- Dietary Fiber: 2g
- Sugars: 3g
- Protein: 15g

This Buffalo Mozzarella, San Marzano Tomato & Basil dish is a tantalizing tribute to the renowned flavors of Tom Douglas's Serious Pie restaurant – a culinary experience that marries simplicity with sophistication. Enjoy the melding of fresh ingredients and bold spices for a truly delightful dining experience.

81. Wild Mushrooms with Truffle Cheese with Chili Flakes & Olive Oil & Basil

Indulge in the earthy richness of wild mushrooms elevated by the luxurious flavor of truffle cheese, heightened with a hint of spice from chili flakes, and adorned with the aromatic essence of fresh basil. Inspired by the culinary marvels at Tom Douglas's Serious Pie restaurant, this dish is a celebration of bold flavors and exquisite ingredients. It's a symphony for the taste buds, combining the essence of the wild with the sophistication of truffle-infused cheese.

Serving: Serves 4
Preparation Time: 20 minutes
Ready Time: 30 minutes

Ingredients:
- 1 pound wild mushrooms (such as chanterelles, morels, or oyster mushrooms), cleaned and sliced
- 200g truffle cheese, grated
- 1 teaspoon chili flakes (adjust to taste)

- 3 tablespoons extra virgin olive oil
- Fresh basil leaves for garnish
- Salt and black pepper to taste

Instructions:
1. Prepare the Mushrooms:
- Clean the wild mushrooms thoroughly and slice them into bite-sized pieces.
- Heat 2 tablespoons of olive oil in a pan over medium heat.
2. Sauté the Mushrooms:
- Add the sliced mushrooms to the pan and sauté until they are golden brown and any liquid released has evaporated.
- Season with salt and black pepper to taste.
3. Add Truffle Cheese:
- Sprinkle the grated truffle cheese over the sautéed mushrooms, allowing it to melt and coat the mushrooms evenly.
- Stir gently until the cheese is melted and forms a creamy coating on the mushrooms.
4. Introduce Chili Flakes:
- Sprinkle chili flakes over the mushrooms and cheese mixture, adjusting the quantity based on your spice preference.
- Continue to stir, ensuring the chili flakes are evenly distributed.
5. Finish with Olive Oil and Basil:
- Drizzle the remaining tablespoon of olive oil over the dish, giving it a glossy finish.
- Tear fresh basil leaves and scatter them over the mushrooms for a burst of herbal aroma.
6. Serve:
- Transfer the wild mushrooms with truffle cheese to a serving platter.
- Garnish with additional basil leaves if desired.

Nutrition Information:
(Note: Nutritional values may vary based on specific ingredients and portion sizes. The values provided are approximate.)
- Calories per serving: 250 kcal
- Protein: 12g
- Fat: 18g
- Carbohydrates: 10g
- Fiber: 3g
- Sugar: 2g

- Sodium: 400mg

Embrace the gourmet allure of this wild mushroom dish, a homage to the inspired creations found at Tom Douglas's Serious Pie. With a perfect balance of earthy, creamy, and spicy notes, this recipe invites you to savor the extraordinary flavors crafted by one of the culinary world's maestros.

82. Soft Farm Egg, Prosciutto, Arugula & Pecorino with Olive Oil & Chili Flakes & Basil

Indulge in the exquisite flavors inspired by Tom Douglas's Serious Pie restaurant with this delectable recipe for Soft Farm Egg, Prosciutto, Arugula & Pecorino, elevated with a drizzle of Olive Oil, a kick of Chili Flakes, and the fragrant essence of Basil. This dish embodies the restaurant's commitment to quality ingredients and inventive combinations that delight the palate.

Serving: Serves 2
Preparation Time: 15 minutes
Ready Time: 20 minutes

Ingredients:
- 4 fresh farm eggs
- 4 slices of high-quality prosciutto
- 2 cups fresh arugula, washed and dried
- 1/2 cup Pecorino cheese, shaved
- 2 tablespoons extra virgin olive oil
- 1/2 teaspoon chili flakes (adjust to taste)
- Fresh basil leaves for garnish
- Salt and black pepper to taste

Instructions:
1. Soft Farm Eggs:
- Bring a pot of water to a gentle simmer.
- Crack each egg into a small bowl.
- Create a gentle whirlpool in the simmering water and carefully slide the egg into the center. Poach for about 3 minutes for a soft, runny yolk.

- Remove the eggs with a slotted spoon and place them on a plate lined with paper towels. Season with salt and pepper.
2. Assembling:
- Lay out the prosciutto slices on serving plates.
- Arrange a handful of arugula on top of the prosciutto.
- Gently place a soft poached egg on each plate.
- Sprinkle shaved Pecorino over the arugula and eggs.
3. Finishing Touches:
- Drizzle extra virgin olive oil over each plate.
- Sprinkle chili flakes for a hint of heat.
- Garnish with fresh basil leaves.
4. Serve:
- Serve immediately, allowing the warmth of the eggs to slightly wilt the arugula and melt the Pecorino.

Nutrition Information:
Note: Nutrition information is approximate and may vary based on specific ingredients used.
- Calories: 350 per serving
- Protein: 18g
- Fat: 28g
- Carbohydrates: 2g
- Fiber: 1g
- Sugar: 0g
- Sodium: 800mg
Experience the harmonious blend of textures and flavors in this Soft Farm Egg, Prosciutto, Arugula & Pecorino dish—a culinary homage to the creativity found at Tom Douglas's Serious Pie.

83. Anchovy & Soft Farm Egg with Tomato Sauce & Chili Flakes with Olive Oil & Basil & Parsley

Indulge your taste buds with a delectable fusion of flavors inspired by Tom Douglas's renowned Serious Pie restaurant. This Anchovy & Soft Farm Egg with Tomato Sauce & Chili Flakes, drizzled with Olive Oil, and garnished with Basil and Parsley promises a symphony of tastes that will elevate your dining experience. Perfect for brunch or a cozy dinner, this dish marries the richness of farm-fresh eggs with the umami punch of anchovies and the warmth of a zesty tomato sauce.

Serving: Serves 4
Preparation Time: 15 minutes
Ready Time: 25 minutes

Ingredients:
- 4 large farm eggs
- 2 tablespoons olive oil
- 4 anchovy fillets, finely chopped
- 2 cups tomato sauce
- 1 teaspoon chili flakes (adjust to taste)
- Salt and black pepper to taste
- Fresh basil leaves for garnish
- Fresh parsley, finely chopped, for garnish

Instructions:
1. Preheat your oven to 375°F (190°C).
2. In a medium-sized skillet, heat olive oil over medium heat. Add the chopped anchovy fillets and sauté until they dissolve into the oil, releasing their savory flavor.
3. Pour in the tomato sauce, add chili flakes, and season with salt and black pepper. Simmer the sauce for 10 minutes, allowing the flavors to meld and the sauce to thicken slightly.
4. Using a spoon, create small wells in the tomato sauce for each egg. Crack an egg into each well, ensuring not to break the yolk.
5. Transfer the skillet to the preheated oven and bake for about 10-12 minutes or until the egg whites are set, but the yolks remain soft.
6. Remove from the oven, and garnish with fresh basil leaves and finely chopped parsley.
7. Drizzle with additional olive oil for a luscious finish.

Nutrition Information:
(Per Serving)
- Calories: 220
- Total Fat: 15g
- Saturated Fat: 3g
- Cholesterol: 195mg
- Sodium: 650mg

- Total Carbohydrates: 12g
- Dietary Fiber: 3g
- Sugars: 6g
- Protein: 10g

Elevate your culinary journey with this Anchovy & Soft Farm Egg creation, a delightful testament to the inspired menu at Serious Pie.

84. Smoked Provolone, Tomato Sauce & Sweet Fennel Sausage with Chili Flakes & Olive Oil & Basil & Parsley

Indulge your taste buds in a symphony of flavors inspired by the renowned Serious Pie restaurant, where culinary innovation meets artisanal craftsmanship. This recipe for Smoked Provolone, Tomato Sauce & Sweet Fennel Sausage Pizza with Chili Flakes, Olive Oil, Basil, and Parsley captures the essence of Serious Pie's commitment to quality ingredients and bold combinations. Elevate your pizza experience with the smoky richness of Provolone, the robust sweetness of tomato sauce, and the savory kick of sweet fennel sausage, perfectly balanced with the heat of chili flakes and the freshness of basil and parsley.

Serving: 4 servings
Preparation Time: 20 minutes
Ready Time: 30 minutes

Ingredients:
- 1 pound pizza dough (store-bought or homemade)
- 1 cup tomato sauce
- 2 cups smoked Provolone cheese, shredded
- 1 cup sweet fennel sausage, cooked and crumbled
- 1 teaspoon chili flakes (adjust to taste)
- 2 tablespoons olive oil
- Fresh basil leaves, for garnish
- Fresh parsley, chopped, for garnish

Instructions:
1. Preheat your oven to 475°F (245°C). If you have a pizza stone, place it in the oven to heat.

2. On a lightly floured surface, roll out the pizza dough to your desired thickness.

3. Transfer the rolled-out dough to a pizza peel or another floured surface that can easily transfer to the oven.

4. Spread the tomato sauce evenly over the pizza dough, leaving a small border around the edges.

5. Sprinkle the shredded smoked Provolone cheese over the tomato sauce, followed by the crumbled sweet fennel sausage.

6. Sprinkle chili flakes evenly over the pizza for a hint of heat.

7. Drizzle olive oil over the top of the pizza, ensuring it reaches the edges.

8. Carefully transfer the pizza to the preheated oven or onto the pizza stone and bake for 12-15 minutes or until the crust is golden brown and the cheese is bubbly and slightly browned.

9. Remove the pizza from the oven and let it cool for a few minutes before garnishing with fresh basil leaves and chopped parsley.

10. Slice and serve hot, savoring the delicious blend of flavors.

Nutrition Information:
(Per serving)
- Calories: 450
- Total Fat: 22g
- Saturated Fat: 9g
- Cholesterol: 40mg
- Sodium: 980mg
- Total Carbohydrates: 42g
- Dietary Fiber: 2g
- Sugars: 4g
- Protein: 18g

Note: Nutrition Information is approximate and may vary based on specific ingredients used. Adjust quantities to meet dietary preferences and restrictions.

85. Guanciale, Castelvetrano Olives & Tomato Sauce with Chili Flakes & Olive Oil & Basil & Parsley

Indulge your senses in the culinary artistry inspired by Tom Douglas's Serious Pie restaurant with this exquisite recipe—Guanciale,

Castelvetrano Olives & Tomato Sauce with Chili Flakes, Olive Oil, Basil & Parsley. This dish harmoniously combines the richness of guanciale, the brininess of Castelvetrano olives, and the vibrant flavors of tomato sauce, chili flakes, olive oil, basil, and parsley. Each bite is a symphony of textures and tastes that will transport you to the heart of Serious Pie's kitchen.

Serving: 4 servings
Preparation Time: 15 minutes
Ready Time: 40 minutes

Ingredients:
- 1/2 cup guanciale, thinly sliced
- 2 tablespoons olive oil
- 1 cup Castelvetrano olives, pitted and halved
- 2 cups tomato sauce (homemade or store-bought)
- 1 teaspoon chili flakes (adjust to taste)
- Salt and black pepper to taste
- 1/4 cup fresh basil, chopped
- 2 tablespoons fresh parsley, chopped
- 1 pound pasta of your choice (spaghetti or bucatini work well)

Instructions:
1. Cook Guanciale:
- In a large skillet over medium heat, add the thinly sliced guanciale and cook until it becomes crispy and golden brown. This usually takes about 5-7 minutes. Remove the guanciale from the skillet and set it aside.
2. Prepare Pasta:
- Meanwhile, cook the pasta according to the package instructions in a large pot of salted boiling water. Drain and set aside.
3. Make Olive Oil Infusion:
- In the same skillet used for guanciale, add olive oil and heat it over medium heat. Add chili flakes and let them infuse the oil for about 1-2 minutes.
4. Combine Ingredients:
- Add Castelvetrano olives to the skillet, followed by tomato sauce. Season with salt and black pepper to taste. Allow the sauce to simmer for 10-15 minutes to meld the flavors.
5. Assemble Dish:

- Add the cooked pasta to the skillet, tossing it in the flavorful sauce. Ensure each strand is coated evenly. Fold in the crispy guanciale, chopped basil, and parsley.
6. Serve:
- Plate the pasta, drizzling with extra olive oil if desired. Garnish with additional fresh herbs and chili flakes for a burst of color and flavor.

Nutrition Information:
Note: Nutrition information is per serving.
- Calories: 500
- Protein: 15g
- Carbohydrates: 65g
- Fat: 20g
- Saturated Fat: 5g
- Fiber: 6g
- Sugar: 8g
- Sodium: 800mg
Elevate your home cooking with this tantalizing dish that encapsulates the essence of Serious Pie's inventive menu. Enjoy the rich interplay of ingredients and savor the gourmet experience in the comfort of your own kitchen.

86. Yukon Gold Potato, Rosemary & Caciocavallo with Olive Oil & Chili Flakes & Basil & Parsley

Indulge in the rustic charm of Yukon Gold potatoes combined with the robust flavors of rosemary, Caciocavallo cheese, and the kick of chili flakes, all drizzled with olive oil and adorned with the freshness of basil and parsley. Inspired by the artisanal creations at Tom Douglas's Serious Pie restaurant, this dish marries simplicity with sophistication, offering a delightful blend of textures and tastes.

Serving: Serves: 4
Yield: 4 servings as a side dish
Preparation Time: 15 minutes
Ready Time: Cook: 40 minutes
Total: 55 minutes

Ingredients:
- 1 1/2 pounds Yukon Gold potatoes, scrubbed and sliced into 1/4-inch rounds
- 3 tablespoons olive oil
- 2 tablespoons fresh rosemary leaves, chopped
- 1 cup Caciocavallo cheese, shredded
- 1 teaspoon chili flakes
- Salt to taste
- Freshly ground black pepper to taste
- Fresh basil leaves, thinly sliced, for garnish
- Fresh parsley, chopped, for garnish

Instructions:
1. Preheat Oven: Preheat your oven to 400°F (200°C).
2. Prepare Potatoes: In a large bowl, toss the Yukon Gold potato slices with olive oil, chopped rosemary, chili flakes, salt, and black pepper until evenly coated.
3. Layer and Bake: Arrange the seasoned potato slices in an even layer on a baking sheet lined with parchment paper or lightly greased. Bake in the preheated oven for 25-30 minutes or until the potatoes are golden brown and tender.
4. Add Cheese: Sprinkle the shredded Caciocavallo cheese over the baked potatoes and return to the oven for an additional 5-7 minutes or until the cheese melts and starts to bubble.
5. Garnish and Serve: Once done, remove from the oven and let it cool slightly. Garnish with thinly sliced basil leaves and chopped parsley before serving.

Nutrition Information:
Note: Nutritional values are approximate and may vary based on ingredients used.
- Calories: 320 kcal
- Fat: 18g
- Saturated Fat: 7g
- Cholesterol: 25mg
- Sodium: 250mg
- Potassium: 800mg
- Carbohydrates: 30g
- Fiber: 4g
- Sugar: 2g

- Protein: 10g
Percent Daily Values are based on a 2000 calorie diet.
This Yukon Gold Potato, Rosemary & Caciocavallo with Olive Oil & Chili Flakes & Basil & Parsley dish captures the essence of comfort and elegance on one plate. Whether as a side or a standalone delight, it promises to tantalize the taste buds and elevate any meal.

87. Penn Cove Clams with House Pancetta & Lemon with Chili Flakes & Olive Oil & Basil & Parsley

Penn Cove Clams with House Pancetta & Lemon, infused with chili flakes, olive oil, and fresh herbs like basil and parsley, are a culinary delight inspired by the vibrant menu of Tom Douglas's Serious Pie restaurant. This dish showcases the harmonious blend of flavors from the sea, the earthy richness of pancetta, and the brightness of citrus and herbs, creating a symphony of taste that's both comforting and sophisticated.

Serving: Serves: 4
Serve these delectable clams as an appetizer or main course with crusty bread to soak up the flavorful broth.
Preparation time: 15 minutes
Ready time: 30 minutes

Ingredients:
- 2 pounds fresh Penn Cove clams, cleaned
- 4 ounces house pancetta, diced
- 2 tablespoons extra-virgin olive oil
- Zest and juice of 1 lemon
- 2 cloves garlic, minced
- 1 teaspoon chili flakes (adjust to taste)
- 1/4 cup chopped fresh basil leaves
- 1/4 cup chopped fresh parsley leaves
- Salt and black pepper to taste

Instructions:

1. Heat a large, heavy-bottomed pot or skillet over medium heat. Add the diced pancetta and cook until it turns golden and crisp, about 5 minutes.
2. Remove excess fat if necessary, leaving about a tablespoon in the pot. Add the minced garlic and chili flakes to the pot, sautéing for a minute until fragrant.
3. Increase the heat to medium-high. Add the cleaned clams to the pot along with the olive oil, lemon zest, and half of the lemon juice. Cover the pot and cook for 5-7 minutes, shaking the pot occasionally, until the clams have opened. Discard any unopened clams.
4. Once the clams are cooked, remove the pot from heat. Taste the broth and adjust the seasoning with salt, pepper, and more lemon juice if desired.
5. Stir in the chopped basil and parsley, reserving a bit for garnish.
6. Ladle the clams and broth into serving bowls. Garnish with the remaining fresh herbs and a drizzle of extra-virgin olive oil.

Nutrition Information:
Nutritional values may vary based on specific ingredients used.
Calories: approximately 250 per serving
Fat: 12g
Cholesterol: 45mg
Sodium: 700mg
Carbohydrates: 10g
Fiber: 1g
Protein: 25g

88. Prosciutto, Pecorino & Arugula with Olive Oil & Chili Flakes & Basil & Parsley

This vibrant dish encapsulates the essence of simplicity and sophistication—drawing inspiration from the gourmet offerings of Tom Douglas's Serious Pie restaurant. The marriage of salty prosciutto, robust pecorino, peppery arugula, and a symphony of aromatic herbs and spices creates a tantalizing melody for the taste buds. Drizzled with olive oil and adorned with chili flakes, basil, and parsley, this dish embodies the culinary finesse synonymous with Serious Pie.

Serving: 2 servings

Preparation time: 10 minutes
Ready time: 10 minutes

Ingredients:
- 6 slices of prosciutto
- 1 cup fresh arugula leaves
- 1/2 cup shaved pecorino cheese
- 2 tablespoons extra-virgin olive oil
- 1/4 teaspoon chili flakes
- Fresh basil leaves, for garnish
- Fresh parsley, for garnish

Instructions:
1. Prepare the Ingredients:
- Lay out the prosciutto slices on a serving platter or individual plates.
- Scatter the fresh arugula leaves evenly over the prosciutto.
- Generously sprinkle the shaved pecorino cheese over the arugula.
2. Drizzle with Olive Oil and Spice:
- Drizzle the extra-virgin olive oil over the assembled prosciutto, arugula, and pecorino.
- Sprinkle the chili flakes evenly to add a hint of heat to the dish.
3. Garnish:
- Tear fresh basil leaves and scatter them on top for a burst of herbal fragrance.
- Finely chop fresh parsley and sprinkle it over the dish for a pop of color and added freshness.
4. Serve:
- Serve immediately and enjoy the harmonious blend of flavors and textures.

Nutrition Information: *(per serving)*
- Calories: 250
- Total Fat: 18g
- Saturated Fat: 6g
- Trans Fat: 0g
- Cholesterol: 40mg
- Sodium: 780mg
- Total Carbohydrates: 2g
- Dietary Fiber: 0g
- Sugars: 0g

- Protein: 18g
Note: Nutrition Information may vary based on specific brands and quantities used.
This delightful assembly of Prosciutto, Pecorino & Arugula with Olive Oil & Chili Flakes & Basil & Parsley embodies the elegance and simplicity of the offerings at Tom Douglas's Serious Pie, inviting you to savor every bite in a symphony of flavors.

89. Buffalo Mozzarella with Tomato Sauce & Basil with Chili Flakes & Olive Oil & Basil & Parsley

This dish draws inspiration from the delightful flavors served at Tom Douglas's Serious Pie restaurant. The combination of creamy buffalo mozzarella, tangy tomato sauce, aromatic basil, a hint of chili flakes, and a drizzle of olive oil creates a harmonious and satisfying dish that celebrates the essence of Italian cuisine.

Serving: - Serves: 4
- Serving Size: 1 portion
Preparation Time: - Prep: 15 minutes
Ready Time: - Ready in: 20 minutes

Ingredients:
- 4 large slices of buffalo mozzarella
- 2 cups tomato sauce
- 1 teaspoon chili flakes
- 4 tablespoons extra-virgin olive oil
- Fresh basil leaves, for garnish
- Fresh parsley, finely chopped, for garnish
- Salt and pepper to taste

Instructions:
1. Prepare the Ingredients:
- Ensure the buffalo mozzarella slices are at room temperature.
- If using store-bought tomato sauce, warm it in a saucepan over low heat. If making homemade sauce, prepare it beforehand.
2. Heat the Tomato Sauce:

- In a saucepan over medium heat, warm the tomato sauce until it's heated through. Season with salt and pepper to taste.
3. Plate the Buffalo Mozzarella:
- Place a slice of buffalo mozzarella on each serving plate.
4. Top with Tomato Sauce:
- Spoon a generous amount of warmed tomato sauce over each slice of mozzarella.
5. Sprinkle with Chili Flakes:
- Sprinkle a pinch of chili flakes over the tomato sauce on each plate. Adjust the amount based on your desired level of spiciness.
6. Drizzle with Olive Oil:
- Drizzle 1 tablespoon of extra-virgin olive oil over each serving.
7. Garnish:
- Tear fresh basil leaves and scatter them over the buffalo mozzarella. Sprinkle chopped parsley on top for added freshness.
8. Serve:
- Serve immediately while the buffalo mozzarella is still warm and gooey.

Nutrition Information (per serving):
- Calories: Approximately 320
- Total Fat: 25g
- Saturated Fat: 9g
- Trans Fat: 0g
- Cholesterol: 30mg
- Sodium: 680mg
- Total Carbohydrate: 10g
- Dietary Fiber: 2g
- Sugars: 6g
- Protein: 14g
Nutritional values are approximate and may vary depending on the specific brands and quantities used.
This buffalo mozzarella dish with tomato sauce, basil, chili flakes, and olive oil embodies the richness of flavors found at Tom Douglas's Serious Pie. Enjoy the creamy, tangy, and aromatic combination that makes for a truly delightful dining experience.

90. Soft Farm Egg, Guanciale & Grana Padano with Olive Oil & Chili Flakes & Basil & Parsley

Indulge in the culinary symphony inspired by Tom Douglas's Serious Pie restaurant with our Soft Farm Egg, Guanciale & Grana Padano creation. This exquisite dish harmonizes the rich creaminess of farm-fresh eggs, the savory allure of Guanciale, the bold notes of Grana Padano, and the tantalizing heat of chili flakes. Finished with a drizzle of olive oil and adorned with fresh basil and parsley, this recipe elevates the classic breakfast egg to a gourmet delight.

Serving: 2 servings
Preparation Time: 15 minutes
Ready Time: 20 minutes

Ingredients:
- 4 farm-fresh eggs
- 100g Guanciale, thinly sliced
- 50g Grana Padano, shaved
- 2 tablespoons olive oil
- 1 teaspoon chili flakes
- Fresh basil leaves, for garnish
- Fresh parsley, finely chopped, for garnish
- Salt and pepper to taste

Instructions:
1. Prepare the Guanciale: In a skillet over medium heat, cook the thinly sliced Guanciale until crispy. Remove from the pan and drain on paper towels.
2. Soft Farm Eggs: While the Guanciale is cooking, bring a pot of water to a gentle simmer. Crack each farm-fresh egg into a small bowl. Create a gentle whirlpool in the simmering water and carefully slide each egg into the center. Poach the eggs for about 3-4 minutes or until the whites are set but the yolks remain runny.
3. Assemble the Dish: Place the poached eggs on serving plates. Distribute the crispy Guanciale around the eggs. Sprinkle Grana Padano shavings over the eggs and Guanciale.

4. Add Flavorful Accents: Drizzle each plate with olive oil, ensuring it cascades over the eggs. Sprinkle chili flakes for a hint of heat. Garnish with fresh basil leaves and a sprinkle of finely chopped parsley.
5. Season to Perfection: Season the dish with salt and pepper to taste.
6. Serve Immediately: This dish is best enjoyed promptly while the eggs are still warm and the flavors are at their peak.

Nutrition Information:
Note: Nutritional values are approximate and may vary based on specific ingredients used.
- Calories per serving: 350
- Protein: 20g
- Fat: 28g
- Carbohydrates: 2g
- Fiber: 0.5g
- Sugar: 0g
- Sodium: 550mg
Elevate your breakfast or brunch experience with this sophisticated yet approachable recipe that captures the essence of Tom Douglas's Serious Pie restaurant.

91. Sweet Fennel Sausage with Roasted Red Pepper & Pecorino with Chili Flakes & Olive Oil & Basil & Parsley

This delectable dish is a fusion of flavors inspired by the renowned menu of Tom Douglas's Serious Pie restaurant. The sweet fennel sausage provides a savory base complemented by the smoky sweetness of roasted red peppers. Topped with zesty pecorino, a hint of chili flakes, fragrant olive oil, and a sprinkle of fresh basil and parsley, this dish offers a symphony of tastes that delight the palate.

Serving: - Serves: 4
- Serving size: 1 sausage link with toppings
Preparation Time: - 15 minutes
Ready Time: - 45 minutes

Ingredients:

- 4 sweet fennel sausages
- 2 roasted red peppers, sliced into strips
- ½ cup grated pecorino cheese
- 1 teaspoon chili flakes
- 2 tablespoons extra-virgin olive oil
- Fresh basil leaves, chopped
- Fresh parsley leaves, chopped

Instructions:
1. Preheat your oven to 375°F (190°C).
2. Place the sweet fennel sausages on a baking sheet and roast them in the preheated oven for approximately 30-35 minutes or until they're cooked through and golden brown.
3. While the sausages are cooking, prepare the toppings:
- Slice the roasted red peppers into thin strips.
- Grate the pecorino cheese.
- Chop the fresh basil and parsley leaves.
4. Once the sausages are done, remove them from the oven and let them cool slightly.
5. To assemble, place each roasted sausage on a serving plate.
6. Top each sausage with strips of roasted red pepper.
7. Sprinkle the grated pecorino cheese evenly over the peppers.
8. Drizzle each sausage generously with extra-virgin olive oil.
9. Sprinkle a pinch of chili flakes over each sausage, adjusting to taste.
10. Garnish with freshly chopped basil and parsley leaves.
11. Serve warm and enjoy the burst of flavors!

Nutrition Information:
- Nutritional information per serving:
- Calories: Approximately 400
- Total Fat: 30g
- Saturated Fat: 10g
- Cholesterol: 80mg
- Sodium: 1000mg
- Total Carbohydrates: 4g
- Dietary Fiber: 1g
- Sugars: 1g
- Protein: 25g
Please note that the nutritional values are approximate and can vary based on specific brands and quantities of ingredients used.

Enjoy this delightful dish inspired by the flavors of Serious Pie restaurant, perfect for a cozy dinner or a gathering with friends and family!

92. Roasted Chanterelle Mushrooms with Truffle Cheese & Thyme with Chili Flakes & Olive Oil & Basil & Parsley

Inspired by the delectable offerings of Tom Douglas's Serious Pie restaurant, this recipe captures the essence of exquisite flavors and textures. Roasted Chanterelle Mushrooms take center stage, complemented by the luxurious essence of Truffle Cheese, aromatic Thyme, a hint of Chili Flakes, and the freshness of Olive Oil, Basil, and Parsley. This dish harmonizes earthy and savory notes, promising a tantalizing culinary experience.

Serving: 4 servings
Preparation time: 15 minutes
Ready time: 35 minutes

Ingredients:
- 1 pound fresh Chanterelle Mushrooms, cleaned and trimmed
- 4 ounces Truffle Cheese, thinly sliced or grated
- 2 tablespoons Olive Oil
- 1 tablespoon fresh Thyme leaves
- 1 teaspoon Chili Flakes (adjust to taste)
- Salt and freshly ground Black Pepper to taste
- Fresh Basil leaves for garnish
- Fresh Parsley, chopped, for garnish

Instructions:
1. Preheat the oven to 400°F (200°C).
2. In a large mixing bowl, toss the cleaned and trimmed Chanterelle Mushrooms with Olive Oil, Thyme leaves, Chili Flakes, Salt, and Pepper until evenly coated.
3. Spread the seasoned mushrooms in a single layer on a baking sheet lined with parchment paper or aluminum foil.

4. Roast the mushrooms in the preheated oven for about 20-25 minutes, or until they turn golden brown and slightly crispy around the edges.
5. Once roasted, remove the mushrooms from the oven and sprinkle the thinly sliced or grated Truffle Cheese evenly over the hot mushrooms, allowing it to melt slightly from the residual heat.
6. Garnish with fresh Basil leaves and chopped Parsley before serving.

Nutrition Information:
- Serving size: 1/4 of the recipe
- Calories: Approximately 180 calories
- Total Fat: 12g
- Saturated Fat: 5g
- Cholesterol: 20mg
- Sodium: 300mg
- Total Carbohydrates: 10g
- Dietary Fiber: 2g
- Sugars: 3g
- Protein: 10g
Note: Nutrition Information is an approximation and may vary based on specific ingredients used. Adjustments can be made to suit dietary preferences or restrictions.

93. Hazelnut Brown Butter Cake with Caramel Sauce & Whipped Cream & Hazelnuts & Mint

Indulge in the exquisite flavors of Tom Douglas's Serious Pie restaurant with this decadent Hazelnut Brown Butter Cake. A delightful combination of nutty hazelnuts, rich caramel sauce, airy whipped cream, and refreshing mint creates a symphony of flavors in every bite. This dessert embodies the essence of Tom Douglas's culinary artistry and will leave a lasting impression on your taste buds.

Serving: 8 servings
Preparation time: 30 minutes
Ready time: Approximately 1 hour 30 minutes

Ingredients:
For the Hazelnut Brown Butter Cake:

- 1 cup unsalted butter
- 1 cup hazelnuts, toasted and finely ground
- 1 ¼ cups all-purpose flour
- 1 teaspoon baking powder
- ½ teaspoon salt
- 4 large eggs
- 1 ¼ cups granulated sugar
- 1 teaspoon vanilla extract
For the Caramel Sauce:
- 1 cup granulated sugar
- 6 tablespoons unsalted butter, room temperature
- ½ cup heavy cream
For the Whipped Cream & Toppings:
- 1 cup heavy cream
- 2 tablespoons powdered sugar
- ½ cup chopped hazelnuts, toasted
- Fresh mint leaves for garnish

Instructions:
1. Prepare Hazelnut Brown Butter Cake:
- Preheat the oven to 350°F (175°C). Grease and flour a 9-inch round cake pan.
- In a saucepan, melt the butter over medium heat. Continue cooking until the butter turns golden brown and develops a nutty aroma, swirling the pan occasionally. Remove from heat and allow it to cool slightly.
- In a bowl, whisk together the finely ground hazelnuts, flour, baking powder, and salt.
- In a separate bowl, beat the eggs and sugar until pale and fluffy. Add the vanilla extract and gradually stir in the brown butter.
- Gently fold the dry ingredients into the egg mixture until just combined. Pour the batter into the prepared cake pan.
- Bake for 25-30 minutes or until a toothpick inserted into the center comes out clean. Allow the cake to cool in the pan for 10 minutes before transferring it to a wire rack to cool completely.
2. Prepare Caramel Sauce:
- In a heavy-bottomed saucepan, heat the granulated sugar over medium-high heat. Stir occasionally with a wooden spoon until the sugar melts and turns amber in color.
- Carefully add the butter to the melted sugar, stirring continuously until the butter is completely melted and incorporated.

- Slowly pour in the heavy cream while stirring constantly until the sauce is smooth. Remove from heat and let it cool slightly.

3. Whip Cream & Assemble:

- In a chilled bowl, whip the heavy cream and powdered sugar until stiff peaks form.

- To assemble, slice the cooled Hazelnut Brown Butter Cake into portions. Drizzle each slice with warm caramel sauce, dollop with whipped cream, sprinkle with chopped hazelnuts, and garnish with fresh mint leaves.

Nutrition Information: (*Note: Nutritional values may vary; below values are approximate per serving*)

- Calories: 540 kcal
- Fat: 39g
- Saturated Fat: 21g
- Cholesterol: 160mg
- Sodium: 210mg
- Carbohydrates: 45g
- Fiber: 2g
- Sugars: 32g
- Protein: 6g

Enjoy this Hazelnut Brown Butter Cake with its luxurious caramel sauce, airy whipped cream, and delightful hazelnut crunch—a delightful dessert that embodies the culinary essence of Serious Pie's menu.

94. Penn Cove Clams with Garlic, Chili Flakes & Lemon with Olive Oil & Basil & Parsley & Mint

Penn Cove Clams with Garlic, Chili Flakes & Lemon infused with Olive Oil, Basil, Parsley, and Mint is a delectable seafood dish inspired by the flavors of Tom Douglas's renowned Serious Pie restaurant. This recipe encapsulates the essence of Pacific Northwest cuisine, combining the freshness of clams with aromatic herbs and zesty citrus flavors.

Serving: 2-4 servings
Preparation time: 15 minutes
Ready time: 25 minutes

Ingredients:
- 2 pounds Penn Cove clams, scrubbed and cleaned
- 3 tablespoons extra-virgin olive oil
- 4 cloves garlic, thinly sliced
- 1 teaspoon chili flakes (adjust to taste)
- Zest of 1 lemon
- Juice of 1/2 lemon
- 2 tablespoons fresh basil, finely chopped
- 2 tablespoons fresh parsley, finely chopped
- 1 tablespoon fresh mint, finely chopped
- Salt and freshly ground black pepper to taste

Instructions:
1. Prepare Clams:
- Scrub the clams thoroughly under cold running water to remove any dirt or sand.
  Discard any clams that are open or cracked.
- Set aside cleaned clams.
2. Prepare Herb Mixture:
- In a small bowl, combine the chopped basil, parsley, and mint. Set aside.
3. Cooking:
- Heat the olive oil in a large skillet or pot over medium heat.
- Add the sliced garlic and chili flakes, stirring constantly for about 1-2 minutes until the garlic turns fragrant and lightly golden.
4. Add Clams:
- Increase the heat to medium-high and carefully add the cleaned clams to the skillet.
- Toss the clams in the garlic-infused oil until they start to open, usually about 5-7 minutes. Discard any clams that do not open.
5. Season and Finish:
- Once the clams have opened, sprinkle the lemon zest over the clams and squeeze the lemon juice into the skillet.
- Season with salt and freshly ground black pepper according to taste.
- Add half of the herb mixture to the clams, reserving the other half for garnish.
6. Serve:
- Transfer the cooked clams and the flavorful broth to a serving dish.
- Garnish with the remaining herb mixture.

Nutrition Information: (approximate values per serving)
- Calories: 220 kcal
- Total Fat: 11g
- Cholesterol: 55mg
- Sodium: 750mg
- Total Carbohydrate: 7g
- Protein: 20g

Note: Nutritional values may vary based on specific ingredients used and portion sizes.

Enjoy this delightful dish of Penn Cove Clams infused with aromatic herbs and zesty flavors, perfect for a taste of the Pacific Northwest!

95. Finocchiona Salami, Castelvetrano Olives & Tomato with Chili Flakes & Olive Oil & Basil & Parsley & Mint

Indulge in the rustic charm of Tom Douglas's Serious Pie restaurant with this delectable recipe inspired by the menu. The combination of savory Finocchiona salami, plump Castelvetrano olives, and vibrant tomatoes, elevated with a kick of chili flakes and the freshness of basil, parsley, and mint, promises a symphony of flavors that will transport you straight to the heart of Italy.

Serving: Ideal for sharing, this dish serves 4 as an appetizer or 2 as a light meal.
Preparation Time: 15 minutes
Ready Time: 15 minutes

Ingredients:
- 150g Finocchiona salami, thinly sliced
- 1 cup Castelvetrano olives, pitted and halved
- 1 cup cherry tomatoes, halved
- 1/2 teaspoon chili flakes (adjust to taste)
- 2 tablespoons extra virgin olive oil
- 2 tablespoons fresh basil, finely chopped
- 2 tablespoons fresh parsley, finely chopped
- 1 tablespoon fresh mint, finely chopped

Instructions:

1. Prepare the Ingredients:
- Slice the Finocchiona salami thinly.
- Pit and halve the Castelvetrano olives.
- Halve the cherry tomatoes.

2. Assemble the Dish:
- Arrange the Finocchiona salami slices on a serving platter.
- Scatter the halved Castelvetrano olives and cherry tomatoes over the salami.

3. Add Spice:
- Sprinkle chili flakes evenly over the ingredients to add a hint of heat.

4. Drizzle with Olive Oil:
- Drizzle extra virgin olive oil over the entire dish, ensuring an even distribution.

5. Herb Infusion:
- Sprinkle the finely chopped basil, parsley, and mint over the top, allowing the herbs to infuse their fresh flavors.

6. Garnish:
- For a final touch, add a few whole mint leaves and a drizzle of extra virgin olive oil.

7. Serve:
- Serve immediately, allowing guests to savor the vibrant flavors and textures of this delightful dish.

Nutrition Information:

Note: Nutrition information is approximate and may vary based on specific ingredients used.

- Calories per serving: 280
- Fat: 22g
- Carbohydrates: 8g
- Protein: 14g
- Fiber: 3g
- Sugar: 2g

Elevate your culinary experience with this Finocchiona Salami, Castelvetrano Olives & Tomato dish, a homage to the inspired creations of Tom Douglas's Serious Pie restaurant.

96. Buffalo Mozzarella, San Marzano Tomato & Basil with Chili Flakes & Olive Oil & Basil & Parsley & Mint

Indulge in the culinary symphony inspired by Tom Douglas's Serious Pie restaurant with our delectable dish, Buffalo Mozzarella, San Marzano Tomato & Basil with Chili Flakes & Olive Oil & Basil & Parsley & Mint. This dish captures the essence of artisanal flavors and showcases the perfect balance of fresh, high-quality ingredients. Elevate your dining experience with the harmonious blend of creamy buffalo mozzarella, sun-kissed San Marzano tomatoes, fragrant basil, a hint of chili flakes, and a drizzle of exquisite olive oil. This recipe promises a delightful journey through taste and texture, mirroring the sophistication found in the renowned Serious Pie menu.

Serving: 4 servings
Preparation Time: 15 minutes
Ready Time: 15 minutes

Ingredients:
- 1 pound buffalo mozzarella, sliced
- 2 cups San Marzano tomatoes, thinly sliced
- 1 cup fresh basil leaves, torn
- 1 teaspoon chili flakes (adjust to taste)
- 3 tablespoons extra-virgin olive oil
- Fresh parsley, chopped (for garnish)
- Fresh mint leaves (for garnish)
- Salt and pepper to taste

Instructions:
1. Prepare the Ingredients:
- Slice the buffalo mozzarella into even rounds.
- Thinly slice the San Marzano tomatoes.
- Tear the fresh basil leaves.
- Chop the fresh parsley.
- Ensure all ingredients are readily accessible for assembly.
2. Assemble the Dish:
- On a serving platter, arrange the buffalo mozzarella slices and top each with San Marzano tomato slices.

- Sprinkle torn basil leaves over the mozzarella and tomatoes.
- Evenly distribute chili flakes over the dish for a hint of heat.
- Drizzle extra-virgin olive oil generously across the platter.
3. Garnish:
- Sprinkle chopped fresh parsley over the dish for a burst of herbaceous flavor.
- Scatter fresh mint leaves for a refreshing touch.
4. Season to Perfection:
- Add salt and pepper to taste, ensuring a perfect balance of flavors.
5. Serve:
- Present the dish immediately to preserve the freshness of the ingredients.

Nutrition Information:
(Per serving)
- Calories: XXX
- Total Fat: XXg
- Saturated Fat: XXg
- Cholesterol: XXmg
- Sodium: XXXmg
- Total Carbohydrates: XXg
- Dietary Fiber: XXg
- Sugars: XXg
- Protein: XXg

Indulge in this vibrant dish that celebrates the essence of Tom Douglas's Serious Pie restaurant, bringing the flavors of buffalo mozzarella, San Marzano tomatoes, and fragrant herbs to your table. Perfect for any occasion, this recipe promises a culinary journey that captures the spirit of artisanal cuisine.

CONCLUSION

In conclusion, "Serious Pie Creations: A Culinary Journey Through 96 Inspired Recipes from Tom Douglas's Iconic Restaurant Menu" offers a delightful exploration of the culinary wonders that have made Serious Pie restaurant a beacon of gastronomic excellence. With a rich tapestry of flavors, techniques, and inspirations, this cookbook encapsulates the essence of Tom Douglas's culinary prowess and the unique character of Serious Pie.

The journey through the 96 recipes mirrors the diverse and vibrant menu that has become synonymous with Serious Pie. From the first page to the last, readers are taken on a gastronomic adventure that transcends the ordinary, inviting them to recreate the magic of the renowned restaurant in the comfort of their own kitchens.

One of the key strengths of the cookbook lies in its meticulous attention to detail. Each recipe is a testament to the commitment to quality and authenticity that defines Serious Pie. From artisanal pizza creations to innovative small plates, the cookbook encapsulates the restaurant's commitment to fresh, locally sourced ingredients and its dedication to elevating the dining experience.

The diverse range of recipes showcased in the book reflects the eclectic nature of Serious Pie's menu. Whether it's the signature pizzas that have garnered a cult following or the inventive small plates that showcase culinary ingenuity, each recipe is a celebration of flavor and creativity. The cookbook, therefore, becomes more than just a collection of recipes; it becomes a homage to the culinary artistry that has made Serious Pie an iconic establishment.

Beyond the recipes themselves, the cookbook offers valuable insights into the culinary philosophy of Tom Douglas. Readers are treated to anecdotes, tips, and techniques that provide a behind-the-scenes look at the inspiration and dedication that go into crafting each dish. This adds a layer of depth to the cookbook, transforming it into a culinary mentorship that empowers readers to not only replicate the recipes but to understand the principles that underpin Serious Pie's success.

Moreover, the cookbook serves as a bridge between the restaurant and its patrons, extending the communal dining experience beyond the physical confines of Serious Pie. It fosters a sense of connection, allowing readers to become active participants in the culinary legacy of

Tom Douglas. The recipes are not merely instructions; they are invitations to join a community of passionate food enthusiasts who share a common appreciation for exceptional dining.

In essence, "Serious Pie Creations" is more than a cookbook; it is a culinary odyssey that captures the spirit of Serious Pie. Through its pages, readers embark on a journey that goes beyond the kitchen, transcending the boundaries of ordinary cookbooks. It is a celebration of creativity, flavor, and the joy of sharing exceptional food with loved ones. As readers delve into the recipes and immerse themselves in the world of Serious Pie, they discover not just a collection of dishes but a profound appreciation for the artistry that defines Tom Douglas's iconic restaurant.

Made in United States
Troutdale, OR
01/03/2025

27576033R00093